Listen, Validate, & Connect

Communication Techniques for Establishing Strong Relationships

Sidney Neel

© **Copyright 2023 - All rights reserved.**

The content contained within this book may not be reproduced, duplicated or transmitted without direct written permission from the author or the publisher.

Under no circumstances will any blame or legal responsibility be held against the publisher, or author, for any damages, reparation, or monetary loss due to the information contained within this book, either directly or indirectly.

Legal Notice:

This book is copyright protected. It is only for personal use. You cannot amend, distribute, sell, use, quote or paraphrase any part, or the content within this book, without the consent of the author or publisher.

Disclaimer Notice:

Please note the information contained within this document is for educational and entertainment purposes only. All effort has been executed to present accurate, up to date, reliable, complete information. No warranties of any kind are declared or implied. Readers acknowledge that the author is not engaged in the rendering of legal, financial, medical or professional advice. The content within this book has been derived from various sources. Please consult a licensed professional before attempting any techniques outlined in this book.

By reading this document, the reader agrees that under no circumstances is the author responsible for any losses, direct or indirect, that are incurred as a result of the use of the information contained within this document, including, but not limited to, errors, omissions, or inaccuracies.

Table of Contents

INTRODUCTION 1

CHAPTER 1: THE BASICS OF COMMUNICATION 3
    WHAT IS COMMUNICATION? 4
    COMMUNICATION METHODS/TYPES 5
        Verbal Methods of Communication 5
        Non-Verbal or Body Language 7
        Professional or Formal Communication 10
        Casual or Informal Communication 11

CHAPTER 2: UNHELPFUL COMMUNICATION HABITS 13
    BAD COMMUNICATION HABITS 14
        Ineffective Listening Skills 15
        Lack of Interest in What's Being Said 16
        Invalidating Someone's Thoughts and Feelings 17
    HOW MISUNDERSTANDINGS HAPPEN IN CONVERSATIONS 18
        Resisting Different in Perspectives 18
        Misinterpreting Non-Verbal Cues 19
        Cultural and Language Barriers 19
        Psychological or Emotional Differences 20
    THE DISADVANTAGES OF POOR COMMUNICATION 21
        Interpersonal Conflict and Relationship Breakdowns 21
        Emotional Turmoil 21

CHAPTER 3: GOOD COMMUNICATION IS THE HEART OF CONNECTION 23
    TWO PILLARS FOR GOOD COMMUNICATION 24
        What Is Emotional Intelligence? 25
        What Is Empathy? 27
    HOW TO IMPROVE YOUR EMPATHY AND EMOTIONAL INTELLIGENCE 30
        Be a Better Listener 30
        Be Open-Minded to Another's Perspective 31
        Learn How to Compromise 31
        Be Kind, Intentionally 32
    THE ADVANTAGES OF GOOD COMMUNICATION 32
        It Sets the Foundation for Strong Relationships 33
        It Improves Problem-Solving Skills for Conflict Resolution 33
        It Boost Self-Awareness 33

It Cultivates Trust *34*

CHAPTER 4: WHAT IS COMMUNICATION IN PROFESSIONAL SETTINGS?...........35

WORKPLACE COMMUNICATION METHODS 36
WHY IS GOOD PROFESSIONAL COMMUNICATION IMPORTANT? 39
It's a Desirable Skill...*39*
It Improves Teamwork and Effort...*40*
It Increase Productivity...*40*
It Minimizes Workplace Conflicts *41*
It Encourages Loyalty and Collaboration..*41*
HOW TO IMPROVE WORKPLACE COMMUNICATION 42
Embrace Feedback *43*
Show Willingness to Learn From Others..*43*
Stay Engaged and Think Before Responding *44*
Make Things Simple *44*
HOW TO EFFECTIVELY COMMUNICATE IN REMOTE WORKSPACES 45
Participate and Clarify Your Expectations *45*
Restore Person-to-Person Communication..*46*
Keep a Schedule and Focus on Performance *47*
Engage in Casual Interactions in the Workplace *47*

CHAPTER 5: COMMUNICATION IN PERSONAL SETTINGS.......................................49

HOW TO MAKE YOUR FRIENDS AND LOVED ONE'S FEEL SAFE DURING CONVERSATIONS......50
Be Vulnerable: Share Your Emotions and Thoughts *50*
Be Compassionate: Avoid Using Absolutes...*51*
Be Considerate: Speak to Others How You Want to Be Spoken to *53*
Be Curious: Seek to Understand Another's Perspective................................*54*
Be Generous: Allow Yourself and the Other Person Ample Time to Share ...*54*
Be Level-Headed: Being Overly Emotional Can Ruin Hinder Communication
....*55*
HOW TO SHOW YOUR LOVED ONE'S THAT YOU APPRECIATE THEM 56
Check-In, Don't Check-Out..*56*
Spend Quality Time With Your People *57*
Give Grace *57*

CHAPTER 6: SOCIAL ANXIETY AND COMMUNICATION 59

TYPICAL MANIFESTATIONS OF SOCIAL ANXIETY 60
The Fear of Judgment...*60*
Intrusive Thoughts and Overthinking *61*
THE IMPLICATIONS OF SOCIAL ANXIETY ON RELATIONSHIPS 61
WHEN SOCIAL ANXIETY BECOMES A DISORDER 62
OVERCOMING SOCIAL ANXIETY—A STEP TOWARDS BETTER COMMUNICATION 63
Exercise, Eat, and Keep Healthy Habits *64*
Thought Journaling...*65*

Practice Exercises for Relaxation *65*
Stop Assuming *70*

CHAPTER 7: DAILY TECHNIQUES FOR EFFECTIVE COMMUNICATION 71

Why Bother Communicating Effectively? 72
Communication Techniques for You 72
Be Clear *74*
Practice Proactive Listening and Responsiveness *74*
Be Attentive to Non-Verbal Cues *75*
Extend Empathy *76*
Be Open to Receiving and Giving Feedback *76*
Validate *76*
How to Improve Everyday Communication 78
Create Chances for Communication by Limiting Your Avoidance *78*
Consider Your Tone *79*
Practice Emotional Intelligence *80*

CHAPTER 8: HOW SELF-CARE CAN HELP YOU COMMUNICATE AND BUILD STRONGER CONNECTIONS 81

Start With Self-Care 82
Self-Awareness Begins When You Communicate Yourself to You *83*
Establish Healthy Boundaries *86*
Get Restful Sleep *88*
Start Meditating *88*
Validate and Connect With Yourself: Fostering a Healthy Self-Image Through Positive Self-Talk 89
All That You Are Influences Your Relationships 91

CONCLUSION 93

REFERENCES 95

Introduction

If you've ever been on the other end of a conversation thinking "How did I interpret that so incorrectly?" or "It's hard not to feel judged in this moment", you aren't alone. When it comes to communication it's easy to lose the essence of the message from both (or more) sides of the conversation to the point where we end up speaking to one another in unconstructive ways. Sometimes you'll even avoid having conversations altogether. Yet, communication will either make or break the quality of your life. What you say, how you say it, and if you say anything at all will fill your life experiences and affect the feelings that people have about you. Subsequently, you need to have a better attitude toward improving your communication style, especially if you're looking to foster healthy and strong relationships with others.

The best way to establish strong connections and ensure that your needs are fulfilled is to build a beneficial way to communicate. The act of effective communication provides you with the platform you need to share your vulnerabilities and needs with the people around you, and doing so will only enhance the value of your interpersonal interactions. When you can respectfully, confidently, and openly share your thoughts you will reduce the chances of ending up in confusing situations or experiencing explosive misinterpretations. Communication is a two-way process and if used well can help you keep a clear and peaceful state of mind. It takes work and continuous practice to cultivate healthy communication techniques that permit others to feel heard and validated, in the same way that you desire to be heard and validated during a conversation.

Unfortunately, we don't have the luxury to sit back and let our communication skills deteriorate because this is a part of our existence that affects and shapes every aspect of our lives. If we're ineffective communicators, our personal and professional relationships will be negatively impacted. It's better to improve your communication skills early rather than ignore them. The great thing about healthy communication is that we're all capable of it. No special tools or access cards are needed to become a good communicator. Ultimately, our willingness to listen to others and be open to different perspectives is all that's needed to start the journey to effective communication.

As a person who has struggled with communication for the most part of my life, I've learned how valuable it is. Nothing can match the profoundness of being able to express yourself clearly. Ineffective communication is often a sign of a lack of confidence, and that's what I found I struggled with for a long time. It wasn't until I noticed the link between success and effective communication that I began to research social anxiety and how to overcome it. Once I started down the path of improving my communication skills, it was as though the self-doubt and lack of confidence I felt before began to melt away. I went from being too afraid to order a coffee to speaking in front of an audience of strangers who were eager to hear what I have to say. With this book, I want to help you overcome your personal barriers when it comes to communication.

If you're willing to brave the journey, I hope to provide you with effective strategies you can use to improve your communication skills. By the end of the book, you will learn the causes of misunderstandings during conversations while gaining insight into how to avoid these barriers to communication. Through the use of effective communication techniques, I'll teach you how to use your entire body to shape the intention of your message during a dialogue with people; it will help you in both professional and personal settings. You can be a good communicator if you want to put in the effort it takes to transform your attitude. You'll also learn how to listen intentionally, be attentive to the needs of others, and confidently share your perspective with people in a way that benefits your entire life. Good communication will help you to live a fulfilled, clear, and thriving life characterized by strong relationships.

Chapter 1:

The Basics of Communication

The most important thing in communication is hearing what isn't being said. — Peter Drucker

One of the biggest mistakes we make in how we communicate is listening for what we want to hear rather than listening for what isn't being said. Too often, we hear others with defensive ears that are ready to argue, prove a point, stake a claim, or rebuttal. In doing so, we miss out on the significant things that are being communicated to us. We automatically become ineffective listeners if we listen to respond or if our listening is based solely on what we hear instead of everything else that comes with conversation. The principle of communication is understanding that its effectiveness hinges on more than what is being said but also on how it's being said and expressed. It means body language and intonation (in other words: what isn't being said) are critical in guiding the way we interpret what we hear.

Learning how to communicate is crucial because no one goes a single day without using the skill. We share ideas, thoughts, opinions, emotions, and even our attitudes through talking with others. Our experience of day-to-day conversations is hugely dependent on the speakers or senders, as well as the receivers. The type of communication we use at any given moment will be determined by those two things, too. For instance, we're less likely to use personal and emotion-driven communication in the workplace. When we're around family and friends, our communication styles are likely to be more informal, compared to when we're speaking or hearing from employers and clients—where we're more likely to use a more formal and professional style. The way we relay and receive information matters, whether we're in a business setting or at home with the people we love. The things we say and don't say while we are communicating will affect the receiver, so we need to be mindful and purposeful about how we express ourselves every time. With that said, before we explore how to change our communication habits for the better, we should first understand what the concept means. This chapter has the objective of revealing the basic information you need to understand what communication is.

What Is Communication?

The art of communication is best described as the process by which valuable information is exchanged between two or more people through familiar symbols, signs, actions, and language (Zafar, 2019). The essence of communication is in fundamental need to establish a strong connection with those whom we are communicating with. Typically, communication is characterized by how we give and receive messages with the aim of reaching a common resolution or understanding. When we talk to others, the leading intention should be to create a safe environment where mutual listening, interpretation, and comprehension can thrive. Speaking and being heard, as well as listening and understanding, are valuable parts of communication; these convey the level of respect and empathy we have for the person or people who are sharing information with us. Ultimately, the power of communicating is in listening and validating other people more than we need to be heard. When we can give other people the space to speak without interruption or haste, is the moment we will begin to improve the way we communicate. We can be effective or ineffective communicators depending on our willingness to respect what's being expressed by someone else and to hear what isn't being said rather than being defensive about what we *think* is being said. With communication comes a lot of humility and a desire to set individual pride and ego aside, so that objective and unbiased interpretations can be made by all the parties involved.

Listening and validation are integral parts of any interaction. The aim here is to improve these two things and create deep connections in the process. When you listen and validate what someone else is saying, you make them feel comfortable to continue expressing themselves. If applied well, communication can uplift us and those around us by making us feel valued and important. By understanding what isn't being said, we can improve how we listen and interpret others during conversations. As such, we can be more open to feedback and acknowledge its importance. The communication methods provided below are important in shaping our understanding of the many ways in which people can communicate. By taking each of these into consideration, will help us do better in this field.

Communication Methods/Types

Communication is an action that's always present in our lives. Even when we don't want to communicate, we're communicating. The various types of communication methods that are available tend to fit the context and environment we're in. We rarely communicate in the same way through all areas of our lives. Ultimately, our method of self-expression will look different with a business client than it does with a romantic partner. Also, various methods of communication will be more acceptable in certain contexts than they would be in others. For example, being approached with a goofy slap on the back and overly enthusiastic energy by a stranger might be a little inappropriate in comparison to receiving the same gestures from a close friend. Learning the different types of communication can be advantageous to you and your relationships because it will help to keep you out of sticky and unfavorable situations. Expanding your knowledge about communication methods can also improve the way you show up in front of others, from context to context. The most common types of communication are verbal, body language, formal, and informal; each of these are methods that we use every single day. Verbal and body language are the most frequent ones because they fall into formal and informal categories of communication. It's important to understand what these methods entail and how you can improve your self-expression through them.

Verbal Methods of Communication

The first type and most frequently used method is verbal communication. It refers to a person's ability to express themselves with words during one-on-one or group interactions. Verbal communication has been known to be the most widely adhered-to method of expression and connection. The nature of verbal communication is to get the speaker's point quickly with a shorter waiting period for a response from the receiver. This method is important in building strong relationships and developing listening skills. Like all types of communication, verbal expression has to be practiced to become effective.

When it comes to verbal communication you need to pay attention to the words you choose for different conversations and consider how those will impact the person you are talking to. For example, vulgarity in a conversation is likely to convey the limited level of respect that you might have for the receiver. The words you choose to say in a conversation matter as they communicate how you feel and what you're thinking. Words often set the tone for the rest of the conversation. Consider this: If one person says something offensive, it's likely to lead to an unprogressive and confrontational dialogue. To carry a healthy conversation, everyone who's part of the communication should have respectful and intentional attitude. It's also important to acknowledge that many people bring unique perspectives to the conversation, and each person should be given the time to express themselves without haste. Keeping respect at the center of verbal communication is also crucial. You might not always agree with the speaker, and they might not always agree with you, but the truth is you can both learn from one another. So, every conversation should be met with that sort of perspective.

Besides being respectful, listening and validating are also valuable parts of communication. When you can listen and validate someone during a verbal dialogue, it'll likely keep harmony between everyone involved. By doing this, it can look like expressing your understanding between pauses. For example, if someone is speaking to you and you agree with what they are talking about, perhaps you can say something like "agreed" between the pauses while allowing them to still continue with their thoughts. It might also be better not to say anything during a pause, but that would depend on the context of the conversation and the speaker's demeanor. Saying words like "I hear you" or "Help me understand your perspective a bit more" can also be ways of validating a person because these phrases show your interest in what's being communicated. It also conveys your desire to fully understand the other person's perspective. So, if the conversation allows it, don't shy away from using validation to express your interest and ask for clarification. Sometimes a verbal conversation doesn't allow for verbal validation which is where the use of body language comes in.

Non-Verbal or Body Language

People don't always mean what they say. That's why taking cues from their non-verbal expressions is important during a conversation. The use of body language is common for face-to-face interactions. When we are communicating with others, we get to interpret their body language, which can convey whether they are tired, engaged, excited, or even absent-minded. Body language also works a great deal in helping each of us decode what someone is saying by paying attention to what isn't being said. Sometimes people can say something but communicate a whole different thing with their body language. The non-verbal method of communicating is one that needs no words, and is prevalent through intonation, the use of facial expressions, physical closeness or distance, and gestures. These can be explained in the following ways:

Intonation

Intonation commonly refers to the pitch or sound of your voice as you speak. It can have a big influence on how a message is interpreted by the listener. During a conversation, people have the ability to decipher your emotions through the tone of your voice in addition to hearing what you're saying. Being attentive to your voice is like examining your speaking pace, how loudly or softly you talk, your tone and pitch, and the timing of your speech. Additionally, using inflections such as "ahh" or "uh-huh" can also communicate to the listener what it is that your words really mean. Through intonation, you can pick up sarcastic expressions, anger, confidence, and affection, among others. Not only do people recognize a message through intonation, but the facial expressions you use also help to convey the meaning being shared or how the message is received.

Facial expressions

Commonly, the way we truly feel is carried in our facial expressions. By looking at your face, people can tell when you are upset even before anything is communicated. The use of facial expressions is a universal guide for all people in knowing when someone is impressed, happy, angry, confused, irritated, and so on. Typically, we'll take cues from facial expressions and tone about whether someone wants us to be closer or distant from them.

Physical Closeness or Distance

We all have personal space bubbles that we don't let just anyone into because space is a sacred part of human security. If you feel uncomfortable, you're likely to distance yourself from the person causing you discomfort as a way of protecting your space; the same is true in conversation. As people, we dread feeling violated or having our personal space invaded. That's why we create distance to express this. In the same breath, the more comfortable we feel, the likelier we are to establish physical closeness with others. Physical closeness and distance can be used to communicate a variety of non-verbal signals that include affection and consent or rejection and disinterest. Space also lends itself to the gestures that we use to express our desire for closeness or distance.

Gestures

People are more likely to express open gestures with someone who doesn't feel like a threat to their space. For example, if you're interested in the conversation and want to hear more from the speaker, you'd likely show it by opening your arms, nodding, having a smile on your face, or other mannerisms of that nature. Gestures are involuntary parts of our daily lives. These are things that happen without us needing to think about them. Some noteworthy gestures include touch, posture, and eye contact.

For instance, someone passionate about something and feels unheard might use their hands to aid in that expression. Alternatively, someone who regrets hurting another person might lean in and rub their back or shoulder to communicate their compassion. People use the gesture of touch to communicate more than not. The way we greet others by waving or comforting others through a hug can send the message to another person that they are being cared for. Another thing is posture. How you sit or stand as you listen to someone speaking is important. When someone slouches during a significant meeting it means that person isn't really hearing what's being communicated. Gestures can communicate understanding, but they can also communicate disinterest. For example, eye contact can show someone how attentive or indifferent you are to what's being said. If someone is important to you, along with what they're saying, then you'll probably make it a point to maintain good eye contact with them. The way you look at the speaker can convey an array of things to them: If the stare is sharp and your eyebrows are raised, it might communicate your confusion or irritation.

Although the use of eye contact is important in ensuring a comfortable flow of conversation, there are people who might struggle with this gesture due to shyness. It's important to note that the use of gestures will vary from person to person and depend on the appropriateness within different contexts. You might not use the same gestures with your colleagues at work that you would with your family at home. Also, your use of gestures might be different depending on how confident or shy you feel on that day.

Non-verbal communication focuses more on how something is being said rather than what's being said. It's about paying attention to all the accompanying signals for what the speaker is trying to communicate. For example, someone might say "I feel safe" with a strong and certain tone, using bold facial expressions or smiling. They might be completely comfortable with their stance which can show you that what they are saying matches their body language. However, consider someone who verbalizes feeling safe, but all the other signals convey something different. For instance, this person's tone of voice might sound shaky, frightened, or uncertain, and their facial expression could be filled with tears in their eyes. If you look at their posture, it seems distant and almost ready to leave the room—this would communicate the opposite of what's being said. Non-verbal communication is highly about being attentive to what isn't being communicated through verbal expression. It's about noticing what someone is expressing beyond the words being used in the conversation. When considering how to express themselves using verbal and non-verbal language, you'd need to think about the context: Is the environment professional or informal?

Professional or Formal Communication

When considering the context, it's worth highlighting the level of formality, whether formal or informal, as expected in any conversation. A formal context is marked by professionalism, where the use of official forms of communication are expected. The way you speak and interact with your co-workers, business partners, or employers is considered professional communication. When it pertains to professionalism, there's a certain expectation of how you should carry yourself. How you talk in the workplace is incredibly important because it plays a part in the type of service you provide as well as how well you're able to interact with your teammates. Formal expression involves multiple ways of responding and engaging. The use of hand gestures is often beneficial in formal communication because it shows that you're fully engaging with the information being shared (Dickinson & Shipley, n.d.). Gestures also work great during presentations or meetings wherein you're the speaker—movement relays your passion for the topic and can also hold the attention of the listeners.

Written work can also have a formal undertone which makes it a part of formal communication. Some examples of this include emails, meeting notes, proposals, letterheads, memos, reports, and other materials (Zafar, 2019). Born in 1971 emails are still the most prominent form of office communication across the world (Patterson, n.d.). You'd think that no one would struggle with expressing themselves in emails by now, however, most people still do. Drafting an important email is a skill that isn't necessarily taught at schools Yet, learning how to write a professional email is a valuable way to maintain rapport and elevate your formal communication skills. To construct a well-written email, you need to mediate for length, tone, clarity of the message, and solutions. You also must proofread the text before you send it. No one wants to read an email that is too long or too short, rude, listing problems and no solutions, and is misspelled or grammatically confusing. It's important to check your words as if you were processing them in your head before pressing send. A poorly written email can turn potential business away from you. An email that isn't proofread, not cohesive, and not structured well suggests a lack of effort and laziness from the sender.

Poor communication in the corporate world can impact any business in a negative way. Without good formal communication, your business or work could lose support, profit, and attention. It's also easy for a person who lacks professionalism to find it difficult to take on leadership positions at work. If you struggle with effective professional communication skills, it can also be challenging to get the attention of future employers or make a positive impact in your current position. Next, we'll explore informal communication which is typically more comfortable and unrestricted.

Casual or Informal Communication

Informal communication is much easier, it's a method that doesn't require official terms and structures to get the message across. Think of casual communication as a grapevine strategy for interaction, this simply means that it has no set channel for how a message must be shared (Zafar, 2019). Some examples of casual interactions that you might have from day to day can take place on any social media system such as WhatsApp, Facebook Messenger, text message (or SMS), and other forms of communication. When we have a casual dialogue with the people around us, it tends to be less bound by restrictions and more free flowing. For example, when you talk to your family and friends, you're less likely to concern yourself with how you express yourself beyond the point of maintaining respect with them. With casual communication, we are less consumed by performance and more focused on building connections by improving our levels of empathy. Informal communication also tends to be more fun and easygoing, especially with groups of people you know and trust.

Even though informal conversations are largely a part of our personal lives, we can also have moments of casual interactions within the workspace. For example, when co-workers are given a platform through which they can communicate about things that aren't work-related, it's a form of informal talk. Catching up with your workmates or having a laugh about past projects and so forth, turns it into casual conversation. Basically, whenever you aren't expected to keep up a structured demeanor, you are participating in informal dialogue. Casual communication is also a great way to form strong connections with your colleagues, and it helps everyone to get more comfortable working together. Ultimately, permitting colleagues to share something in casual conversations can improve teamwork and performance within the office space. As it turns out, professionalism doesn't mean a lack of friendliness. Hopefully, knowing this will encourage you to extend yourself more within an office setting, and casually start a conversation with people you wouldn't usually do so. Who knows—you might end up making work friends along the way.

Information around the topic of communication isn't without the understanding that we are all unique, and conversations aren't necessarily fun for everyone. I recognize that there are times when causal communication can be anxiety provoking. Typically, it can cause anxiety when you're prompted to speak to a stranger but lack the confidence to do so. In a party or housewarming scenario, for instance, it might be a bit stressful to have to interact in a social setting when personally you only know a few people or no one at all. Having social anxiety is common for those who aren't comfortable being with people they don't know, and it tends to make casual conversations feel like pulling teeth. The concept of social anxiety will be further explored in the upcoming chapters to provide you with a clearer idea of what it means. However, let's take a look at some unhelpful communication habits that might contribute to making conversations slightly more difficult than they need to be.

Chapter 2:

Unhelpful Communication Habits

Constantly talking isn't necessarily communicating. —Charlie Kaufman

Having something to say just to chime into a conversation isn't necessarily a helpful communication habit. Ultimately, communication is more about listening than about speaking, and many of us miss that part. We would rather be the ones talking and being heard or understood instead of prioritizing doing that for someone else. Unhelpful communication habits refer to the unprogressive techniques that we use to communicate with people. We often learn the hard way that we don't have to say everything that comes to mind. The good news is, there are better ways to communicate: Methods that don't involve lashing out, gaslighting, or dismissing what someone else is saying. It's not enough to know that your communication skills will improve if you aren't taking the necessary steps to refine them.

Interpersonal communication isn't always straightforward because we are all different, and those differences come with unique perspectives. When there are diverse points of view and understanding, it can cause friction between the speaker and the listener and vice versa. Too many thoughts, upbringings, beliefs, and ideas can make it challenging to exchange information between people seamlessly and uninterruptedly. When this happens, it can raise some concerns about the way we approach interpersonal dialogues. Many times, people tend to be so focused on getting their individual points across that they forget to stop and consider what the other person's perspective might be. Even when we pause to consider it, our own biases might hinder our ability to absorb the information without disturbing or undermining the person sharing it. As a result, conversations end up being misinterpreted, and the intended message may be received in a different way than the speaker had expected. If only we understood that communication is a collaborative effort, it'd be pointless if those involved in it aren't being respected and listened to.

Learning what some communication barriers are can enhance the conversation enough for all parties to be heard. Multiple factors can fail communication between people. Perhaps, the most powerful way to learn how to communicate effectively is by learning how *not to* communicate ineffectively. In this chapter, the aim is to see where your communication might be lacking so that you can improve in those areas. The information provided here seeks to identify all the ways that a person can be viewed as a "bad" communicator. Being aware of where you fall short is a great step toward transforming how you communicate. This chapter has the primary objective to help you find new ways to explore some of your unhelpful communication habits that might be leaving you low in energy and constantly feeling misheard during conversations.

Bad Communication Habits

Bad communication habits are so real, and we all have them, but they may look different from day to day. These habits keep us from establishing strong connections because they involve either being dismissive, not listening, or not paying attention to the speaker. Bad communication habits make the other person feel alone, unheard, or unsupported during an interaction, which can make it difficult for the conversation to produce anything constructive. A lot of the time, these habits get us into sticky and unfavorable positions with people, leaving one or more individuals feeling discouraged from having future conversations with us. Bad habits in communication can lead to breakdowns in professional and personal relationships. They prevent us from working effectively within team settings, where good communication is the key. Ineffective communication patterns can leave us nowhere further than where we began the conversation. They can also cause friction and misinterpretation between the parties involved. The aim of any good conversation should strive to be attentive, growth oriented, and with the possibility to learn something new. However, ineffective communication habits keep us from attaining those important things. This can leave us stuck with the same ideas and knowledge that we came into the day with. When we can't communicate ourselves to others, it hinders our ability to expand our knowledge.

Think of having a good conversation as your chance to enrich your mind with information that is unique from your own. By participating in healthy interactions, you allow your mind to learn new things which can shape you into a better person and increase your skills as a communicator. However, sometimes we are so stuck in our own perceptions and ideals that we run the risk of indirectly invalidating other people's perspectives. People are territorial beings, and it's no wonder we are so quick to cling to protecting and defending our views rather than conveying a willingness to learn from others. The unwillingness to listen to someone else without interruption basically shows one's lack of desire to learn and grow. That is unfortunate because we stand to win and improve so much more by taking the time to change bad communication habits into being able to carry a constructive conversation.

Understanding what these could be will keep you from experiencing unpleasant encounters with people whose perspectives differ from yours. The first step to unlocking good communication skills is knowing some of the barriers that stop us from communicating effectively, even when the intention to do so is there. Some of the unhelpful habits that will be covered in this section include ineffective listening, lack of interest in what's being said, being distracted, and invalidating someone's feelings during a conversation. Each of these habits will be explored to give you understanding about an issue so that you can change it for the next interaction you'll have.

Ineffective Listening Skills

Improving your listening skills is one significant way to improve your communication. Remember: it's more about listening anyway. Ineffective listening is detrimental to any communication. No one wants to sit through a conversation where they aren't being heard or understood. Also, no one wants to communicate with people when they feel that their message isn't being taken seriously. An example of bad listening is when someone listens in anticipation for the speaker to stop so that they can respond with their own ideas. When people listen with the intention to respond, it usually means that they aren't making much of an internal effort to process the actual message. Instead, they've taken part in their own inner dialogue, formulating all the things that they'll communicate to the speaker when it's their turn to take the floor. Quite frankly, listening to respond conveys a lack of desire to understand what the speaker is sharing. It also suggests that the only ideas that the listener deems valuable are the ones that they'll share with the speaker.

Everyone can fall victim to waiting to speak, rather than to listen and learn. Research studies show that most people only listen with about 25% efficiency (Skills You Need, n.d.). Luckily, we can replace this habit with a more positive one. Next time you find yourself tempted to start an internal dialogue while someone else is sharing their point, take an active pause to ask yourself: What is the speaker saying? What is one good idea that I've heard from the speaker so far? What is one thing that I need clarity about? When you start to employ this tactic during every conversation, you'll begin to notice your listening skills transforming. It will take practice, but developing effective communication skills is worth every bit of effort. So, train yourself to actually listen to what someone is saying, and you'll be pleasantly amazed at what you can learn from others through attentive listening.

Lack of Interest in What's Being Said

Training yourself to listen attentively shows the other person that you're interested in hearing what they have to say. A huge cause of miscommunication and conflict during conversations is showing disinterest in what the speaker is talking about. Lack of interest can manifest in a multitude of ways, one of which is not engaging with the speaker on the information shared. For example, if someone is excited to share something with you and by the end of their talk, the only response you have is "Okay, cool," can be discouraging and communicate that you don't really care. However, if your response is found with curiosity and eagerness to fully embrace that moment with them, it can change the whole dynamic of the interaction. Another thing that can show disinterest is to start talking about something else while the speaker is sharing their perspective. Being on your phone during a conversation is another example of this. It's hard for the speaker to believe that you're engaged in the conversation when something else has your attention more at that moment. If anything, distractions 100 percent communicate indifference. Another example is that during a conversation you do things like yawning, having wandering eyes, fidgeting, checking the time, and being absent-minded. None of these things communicate to the speaker that the listener is interested in listening. If you don't show any signs that you are interested in the message, you're more likely to end up in a situation of conflict and misinterpretation. The inability to pay complete attention during a conversation makes communicating difficult. It can also lead to a breakdown in relations because when people feel like they can't understand each other they're less likely to want to continue with future interactions. A bad communication habit such as this one can leave the other person feeling invalidated and unheard.

Invalidating Someone's Thoughts and Feelings

Making someone feel as though their emotions, thoughts, and experiences don't matter is known as invalidation. When someone doesn't feel valued, it's hard to be expressive or vulnerable, which makes communicating challenging. Saying things like "It's not that important" or "You shouldn't feel this way about this" are overt signs of invalidating someone's ideas and emotions. It isn't a position that you want to be in if you truly care about what the speaker is saying. Invalidating someone occurs when you act dismissively toward what they are communicating. It also happens when you won't let them finish a thought or you shrug off the information, they've shared with you as unimportant. Bad communication habits can cause a wedge between people and leave us feeling low, doubtful, and anxious. At some point in this book, you'll learn techniques to help you become a better communicator, which will hopefully eliminate bad habits.

It's essential to note that some of these *signs* can be a result of other situations that might not be related to disinterest or typical communication behaviors. For example, people with autism and attention deficits might struggle a bit more with interpersonal communication and thus have a higher tendency of showing some of these habits. Someone on the atypical spectrum isn't going out of their way to convey disinterest, so you need to be mindful about that too. Let's take a look at how misunderstandings happen in conversations.

How Misunderstandings Happen in Conversations

When bad communication habits are applied to a conversation it can leave one or more people feeling unheard or misunderstood. When the message is clear to the sender but unclear to the recipient it can cause a major roadblock in communication. Inversely, when the receiver isn't paying attention to the speaker or the speaker feels as though their message is landing on uninterested ears, it can cause problems. In this section we'll explore the common causes for misunderstandings. Getting to know them will help you identify some of the barriers to communication that you might have been experiencing in your life. Knowing some of the barriers can give you insights about taking the first step toward becoming a better communicator.

Resisting Different in Perspectives

Communication is a skill that we use in every corner of our lives; we use it at work, with our families, and in our communities. However, we're bound to have differences in opinions and perspectives because we're unique with subjective views and how we perceive the world. Conversations with our colleagues might not always end with a commonly shared conclusion, and the same is true for conversations we have with our families. Even so, it's important to acknowledge our distinctions and use them to equip us with compassion, willingness, and attention to what others (outside of our view) may have to share. Resisting the differences that exist from person to person is like dismissing valuable and subjective input from one another. It also feels like we're imposing our individual thoughts and perspectives onto the other person, that can cause friction within any relationship. Sometimes different perspectives may come across as threatening to our personal ideologies or viewpoints, thus can cause a fracture in the way we communicate ourselves or receive information from others. It also leads to a significant misinterpretation of what's being said, both verbally and non-verbally.

Misinterpreting Non-Verbal Cues

The gestures and facial expressions that we use during face-to-face interactions are like reading signs that provide deeper insight into what someone is feeling. However, we aren't always correct in how we interpret someone else's demeanor because our biases can pertain to the topic and can easily influence the way we receive information from the speaker. Yet, if we interpret someone else's body language we're more likely to respond through that interpretation which can cause misunderstanding, especially if it's misaligned with their intention. Alternatively, misinterpretation is just as possible in virtual spaces as it is in physical spaces. It means we can just as easily misinterpret a text or call as we can non-verbal cues, we see in the person we are talking to. In texts and calls, we don't get the opportunity to see body language the way we would during a face-to-face conversation. Therefore, the inability to read the room by referencing someone's non-verbal cues can be a barrier to how we communicate. Without body expressions and gestures, we are limited in our assessment of what the speaker is saying and how the recipient or listener is receiving the message. Somehow, misinterpretations are more common in virtual spaces than they are in shared physical spaces. Many misunderstandings can occur because of cultural and language barriers as well.

Cultural and Language Barriers

Perhaps we've been exposed to different things, and ways of speaking mean different things depending on the community we're from. Our background differences and communication styles can be the first cause of misunderstandings. What is honest or direct in some countries might be viewed as rude in others. Depending on how we're raised and what language we speak, some gestures and interpretations can be lost in translation. Some cultures are louder and more expressive than others. Because of that, things could be interpreted negatively in maybe more conservative and stoic cultures. How we see what's respectful and appropriate during a conversation, depends on the influences that we've had throughout our lives, and these influences shape how we process communication. Psychological and emotional understanding also shape our understanding of others' messages.

Psychological or Emotional Differences

As a result of our backgrounds and the influences that shape our cognitive activities, there's a delicate line between understanding what someone is saying or misinterpreting them completely. Miscommunication can happen when people receive the same information but process it differently. Where one person might hear something and cry, another might be frustrated because they don't see a reason for crying in that situation and so on. Our psychological interpretations of what's being said significantly influence our emotional responses in different situations. Think about people who are more temperamental compared to those who are more solution based. Often one feels less understood by the other, that results in tensions and misunderstandings.

Our emotional responses can also cause conflict in relationships because it's easy for emotions to be misinterpreted. For example, an emotion like anger is usually pointing to a deeper feeling that manifests itself. Someone who's sad or upset can easily respond to something in ways that communicate anger, such as wagging their finger and saying something with a bold vocal tone. Also, anger doesn't always lead to volatile behaviors such as screaming or punching stuff. An angry person can also cry as an expression of their frustration. The point is emotions can be experienced on a wide spectrum, and that's what makes it difficult to interpret them. This difficulty can portray major communication issues. In the next section, we'll look at the disadvantages of poor communication in more detail.

The Disadvantages of Poor Communication

When you're communicating with a co-worker or a friend, the last thing anyone wants to experience is bad habits of communication. Being on the receiving end of any of the previously mentioned habits isn't a fun place to be, and it can take its toll on the conversation and the shared connection. That's why it's so important to take the time to learn effective tools that you can use to avoid the pitfalls of poor communication. Besides creating misunderstandings, bad communication habits can also result in interpersonal conflicts, which set the foundation for a breakdown in relationships, among other things.

Interpersonal Conflict and Relationship Breakdowns

Who feels valued in a conversation with no eye contact or reassurance? Literally no one. If you walked into your boss's office or your friend's house with an exciting idea to share, and all you got was "okay," while they gazed out of the window. You'd probably feel slighted. Once you continuously feel unimportant during interactions with people, you develop a sense of self-preservation that tells you to avoid conversations with those people. It means that friends you used to connect with no longer feel like safe spaces, or a colleague you shared thoughts with is no longer reliable. Miscommunication is quick to cause interpersonal conflict, especially since the foundation of any good relationship is connection. Understanding and shared reasoning are the cornerstones of any strong relationship, as without these, feelings of hostility may arise and slowly dissipate people's desire to communicate. Of course, friction from an interpersonal relationship has emotional consequences.

Emotional Turmoil

When you start to drift from a valuable relationship, or you begin to see the end of something that once was good, it can take an emotional toll on you. Also, trying to understand people and constantly misinterpreting them can equally lead to emotional drain. Life can feel overwhelming and hard without understanding and good communication, and it can make people question themselves and others. Once your inner environment is persistently affected by internal dismay, it can increase anxiety and decrease self-confidence. As a result, you're more likely to develop more resilience to expressing yourself in new or even familiar environments. The best way to avoid relationship fractures is by teaching yourself how to communicate in a way that's effective; one which helps you feel confident in expressing yourself, while others can feel heard too. Good communication is the heart of connection, and the following chapter will explore that in more depth.

Chapter 3:

Good Communication is the Heart of Connection

Great communication begins with connection. —Oprah Winfrey

Good communication is important in personal and professional relationships. Learning how to communicate effectively will improve your listening skills and enhance your ability to connect with others. We need to learn how to speak well to prevent conflict and misunderstandings that can make us upset, resent, and confused in relationships. It takes people who are open to learning multiple skills to become good communicators. Since rapport starts with connection, it's important to lean into the practices that support you in building genuine bonds with people. For example, before beginning any form of interaction, set aside any possible distractions that could take your attention away from connecting with the person in front of you.

It's easy to get distracted in this technologically advanced and social media-driven world, but distractions impede our ability to build empathy and form genuine companionship. Our phones, laptops, and even our imaginative minds can be massive distractions and hindrances to communication. When we constantly need to look at our laptops to check on work, it makes us appear preoccupied, which either makes us unapproachable or challenging to hold a conversation with. Even being distracted by email and social media notifications keeps us from stretching our attention toward interacting with others. When we communicate, we tend to say a lot by saying nothing at all. For instance, if you want to talk to someone who continuously cuts you off to attend to a more important alert on their phone, you can become far less encouraged to continue that dialogue.

Adopting healthy communication can help you to concentrate during integral communicative moments so that you can strengthen your connections with others and avoid misinterpretation. Learning how to communicate without distractions is important, which is why I want you to get a full experience of what it means to be an effective communicator. So, this section may be lengthier than the others—so brace yourself. In this chapter, we will explore information that will help you to better understand what good communication is by exploring its two fundamental pillars.

Two Pillars for Good Communication

In the architectural field, pillars provide structural support and foundational assistance to a bigger attachment to guarantee its stability (Khillar, 2018). Pillars prevent the collapse of larger structures and ensure that the integrity of the attachment is upheld. When pillars decay or fall apart, the entirety of the larger attachment is threatened. For example, buildings can't stand without strong pillars in place and even the most solid structures can't withstand pressure if the foundational support is weak. What if we took this perspective and allowed it to influence our understanding of valuable interactions? Let's employ the same or a similar analogy to communication and connection. When the pillars that strengthen our ability to communicate effectively aren't secure, we run the risk of struggling with weakened connections. If our conversational skills have structural support issues, our connections can easily fall apart.

The two main pillars of effective communication are emotional intelligence and empathy, and these elements are integral parts of strong human connection (Goleman, 2006). Without emotional intelligence, it's easy to be clueless about how to interpret non-verbal cues. Someone with low emotional intelligence is less likely to respond appropriately to the emotional climate of a situation. For example, consider being at work. You see your colleague frantically walk out of an important meeting with tearful eyes. At that moment, the emotionally intelligent thing to do would either be to check on your co-worker or give them the space they need to process their feelings. Whereas the emotionally unintelligent thing to do is follow them back to their office to ask them to explain something work-related that you need assistance with. Having empathy and emotional intelligence keeps us from causing psychological harm in situations where it can be avoided. We develop a better read on people and situations that keeps us from making rushed decisions that can cause irreparable damage to others, and to ourselves. By acknowledging empathy and emotional intelligence as foundational support for communication, we can truly begin to understand how the whole structure can crumble if these two components aren't upheld.

What Is Emotional Intelligence?

When we talk about emotional intelligence, we are referring to the set of abilities or skills that people should possess which allow us to form deep understandings with others (Cherry, n.d.). High emotional intelligence helps us become better at regulating our own emotions in different settings to avoid inappropriate behaviors. Being an emotionally intelligent person means that you have developed a strong capacity to notice, interpret, and manage your own feelings so that you're better equipped to hold the same emotional space for others. Emotional intelligence is a social skill that can be sharpened to help us cultivate strong connections and positive interactions. According to author and psychologist, Daniel Goleman, there are five key elements that distinguish an emotionally intelligent person: self-awareness, self-management, social skills, empathy, and determination (Goleman, 2006).

Self-Awareness

Being self-aware refers to our ability to be attentive to our cognitive processes such as our thoughts, moods, and feelings, so we can have a better understanding of our behaviors (Cherry, n.d.). It's about being attuned to the inner self in a way that helps us to recognize the impact of our actions on the communities and people around us. A person who's self-aware is capable of high levels of self-evaluation that permit them to identify emotional stimulation and respond in a way that preserves their relationships. Self-awareness makes us conscious of the link between subjective cognitive processing and behavior. This level of consciousness makes it possible for us to see the world objectively, and from that, we can acknowledge our limitations as well as our strengths without judgment. Self-awareness gives us the opportunity to go out into the world and cultivate authentic relationships that help us to perform at our best. Through this consciousness, we become more open to equipping ourselves with new information by permitting ourselves to learn from others. This makes us ready to receive feedback that may help us improve, without feeling attacked by it. Having consciousness at this level is great because it enlarges our capacity to connect and improves our ability to self-regulate in different situations.

Self-Management

Self-regulation or management refers to our ability to use the awareness that we have of ourselves to cope with the cognitive processes that we experience. Coping with our cognitive processes doesn't mean suppressing our emotions or denying our moods. On the contrary, it means we possess the skill to give ourselves the time that's necessary to process these emotions before we act on them. Self-management is more about putting self-awareness into practice by recognizing when and how to respond to emotional stimuli. It's the ability to know when our responses will be beneficial or harmful to the situation we are dealing with. Regulating yourself provides you with the freedom to express yourself and to do so responsibly. People who effectively regulate their emotions tend to demonstrate high levels of consideration for how their responses and actions will affect others. Therefore, it makes it easier for self-regulated people to develop strong social skills and connections.

Social Skills

Emotionally intelligent people are able to foster strong social ties with others. Social skills are our ability to interact and understand other people. The ability that each person has to connect with others can easily be informed by their self-awareness and regulation. Having nonjudgmental and expressive conversations with people from different schools of thought, can help us to develop valuable social skills that can benefit our personal and professional lives. Being socially skilled means, we can assess non-verbal and verbal cues alike, without imposing our own ideas of how things should be. Essentially, it's being able to allow a natural flow of communication that brings value to yourself and those you're talking to. Our social skills can help us show up for people in empathetic and compassionate ways.

Determination

Another element of emotional intelligence is being determined, which refers to the mental state of being internally encouraged to do something. Being determined conveys a desire to push towards the fulfillment of your goals. It also involves prioritizing internal rewards over external recognition and keep doing great work and being a good friend even in moments when you don't feel like it. Determination is the truest test of character, it's the ability to maintain a resilient attitude even when no one is applauding or congratulating you. Intrinsic motivation is having deeply personal reasons for continuously showing up; reasons that aren't influenced by who see you or how people act toward you. The ability to be action-oriented will guide you to continuously excel and be a better person—and that's the beginning of true empathy.

Empathy

Our responses to what people have communicated guide how well or bad the conversation will go. Empathy is an important aspect of emotional intelligence. It's also a valuable pillar of communication on its own. We'll explore this concept further in the following section.

What Is Empathy?

Empathy is the human ability to see a problem or a situation from someone else's perspective (Schmitz, 2016). It's the awareness of the feelings and emotions shared by others which is an integral skill not only in professional communication but in intimate interactions as well (Orr, 2021). When it comes to communication, empathy is the willingness or desire to understand the thoughts, feelings, and messages that other people share with us. When we're empathetic toward others, we make them feel cared for and that their values matter. Expressions of empathy are important in the conversations and exchanges that we have with people, regardless of a setting. Exercising empathy in daily interactions can lead to high professional achievements, quality interpersonal connections, and improved mental health. Not only do we stand to benefit personally by expressing empathy, but we contribute to making a better world too. Empathy helps to foster positive, open, and vulnerable bonds that give us an opportunity to share our thoughts in trusting relationships, and it also appears to be a foundational part of emotional intelligence. Through empathetic expressions, we gain soft skills such as consciousness of our surroundings, awareness of others, resilience, increased self-confidence, and conflict management (Schmitz, 2016). When we can enhance our empathy, it will take our relationships and connections to a new level. Practicing empathy will elevate your interactions and, in most cases, it will reduce the possibility of conflict where differences in perspective are concerned. Ideally, being empathetic should help us cultivate a sense of mutual understanding, grow together, and celebrate each other's differences.

Shared Understanding

Developing a shared understanding in moments of vulnerability with others is a powerful thing. Empathy empowers us to remain attentive to our emotions as well as to be conscious of subtle emotional cues from the people we're interacting with. Working toward understanding others involves being sensitive to their experiences and perspectives. It's also about being aware that their views may not make sense to you, but they are important to the person sharing them. Cultivating shared understanding also encompasses having the emotional maturity to know that it's better to work towards a common solution than to start conflict. It's about knowing that not all battles are worth the fight and choosing when to put your pride aside for the advancement of the common goal. Having a mutual understanding helps us to grow in our relationships with others because with it, we learn how to be better communicators. Our interpersonal interactions tend to flourish when healthy communication is in play.

Interpersonal Growth

We grow together. Even if we struggle to see where someone else is coming from, our ability to respond with empathy and respect allows us to grow stronger and closer together. Through empathy, we are able to handle the sensitive information that people share with care, even if we don't agree with what they are saying. By communicating empathetically, we give ourselves permission to listen with non-judgmental ears. It means we have a greater opportunity to expand our view on things. When interpersonal growth happens, taking and giving feedback becomes easier, and so does self-expression. There's no point in having conversations between people that don't either teach us something or improve our lives in any way. We can learn plenty of things from one another because of our differences, and those lessons are what lead to growth.

A Celebration of Differences

Diversity is a wonderful thing, as it helps to keep life interesting and enriched with new information. As people, we can never know everything, and we should always be open to learning. We can only improve and become better by making ourselves available to absorb new ideas and perspectives. So, appreciating diverse ways of living, thinking, processing, and interpreting situations is something that should be celebrated often. According to Goleman (2006), our differences are powerful social tools that can be leveraged to create better opportunities that are characterized by varying inputs. In short, celebrating our diversity is an acknowledgment that each of us has unique insights to add to a conversation, and thus we're all valuable. Empathetic people are able to leverage diversity because of this skill. Also, it's easier to respect other people's feelings, experiences, and opinions when recognizing that they are equally important—despite their physical, racial differences. Diversity is a chance to add more information to our knowledge pack, and it provides us with an opportunity to improve our interpersonal skills by putting our biases aside and working to understand diverse mindsets. It strengthens our ability to relate with larger groups of people. So, celebrating differences helps us to change prejudices and challenge injustices when we see them, as to foster a wide range of safe, respectful, and appreciative social spaces. Learning ways to strengthen these two pillars for ourselves will have long-term advantages for our relationships and interactions.

How to Improve Your Empathy and Emotional Intelligence

Mindfulness plays a significant role in empathy and emotional intelligence, it's the ability to practice an awareness of others by recognizing that a moment is more than just about you. This is a great thing but it's not always easy and it doesn't come naturally to most of us. Especially in moments when we feel that we're on the right side of the conversation, and the other person needs to do better. Thankfully, there are multiple ways we can use the knowledge that we have about empathy and emotional intelligence to get better at both.

Be a Better Listener

Listening is a staple in communication. There's no shared understanding or celebration of differences without it. Active listening is also an ongoing process that involves hearing, understanding, recalling, interpreting, evaluating, and responding to what's being said. When you listen to someone, you hear the information that they are sharing, and it means acknowledging what they are communicating. Then you proceed to try and understand why the message is important to the speaker and their reasons for wanting to share it with you. After that, you can recall the information by asking them for clarity on what you think you understand about what they are saying and encourage them to correct you if you are off track. Being curious about the delivered message and working towards acknowledging it will help you better interpret the information. Once you've gone through those steps of active listening, you can then mentally evaluate and process what you'd like to contribute to the dialogue—only after that should you respond.

If you could go into every conversation eager to learn from what someone has to share with you, you'd realize that listening in communication is better than constantly speaking. To improve your empathy and emotional intelligence, you must be willing to listen–there's just no way around that. When you listen intently to someone, they automatically feel accepted, encouraged, and celebrated, which are all important parts of a healthy communication. It doesn't mean you always have to agree with their point of view, but it does mean you need to respect it all the time. Being a better listener is the primary way to establish strong relationships and improve in other areas of your life. You can't grow, evolve, or learn without listening and keeping an open mind.

Be Open-Minded to Another's Perspective

Open-mindedness helps you to enter a conversation with no expectations, which involves leaving your prejudices, assumptions, and biases at the door. Emotional intelligence and empathy are marked by your willingness to hear perspectives that differ from your own and not internalize these as potential attacks. Sharing someone else's perspective doesn't mean you'll have to conform to it. Instead, it's about recognizing that the differences of others are worthy as your own. Open-mindedness makes people feel safe to share their beliefs, and it prevents you from trying to impose your points of view on them. When we're open-minded, communication starts to feel easy because no one's ideas and perspectives are made to feel inferior to another. Open-mindedness is about being considerate of someone else's journey and viewpoints and making an effort to understand them—this is a mark of an empathetic and emotionally aware person.

Learn How to Compromise

Another way to improve your empathy and emotional intelligence is by learning to compromise. It doesn't mean abandoning your own emotions for the sake of agreeing with someone else and always following the other person's lead. Instead, compromise is about sharing information and finding a way to solve a problem so that both or more parties can defuse the situation and reach an understanding and find a solution. It's about creating a safe space where ideas can be joined to make one big thing rather than marginalizing one's perspective in favor of another. Compromise happens from all parties involved, and it's for the benefit of everyone. Also, there can be no compromise in communication if there's no kindness.

Be Kind, Intentionally

Kindness is a huge part of being empathetic because it makes people feel that they are protected and cherished in every conversation. Being kind isn't about agreeing with everything or doing things to make others happy. On the contrary, kindness is acknowledging that there is always a more considerate way of stating the truth, which doesn't involve emotional belittlement or badgering. You can be upfront and confident in your responses and still deliver your message in a way that considers the emotions of others. People prefer the truth to be spoken in a loving way rather than to be told a lie to maintain a false sense of peace. So, find those loving ways to express your interests and disagreements and you'll see magic happen. You need to learn how to keep your energy approachable, yet firm, so the person you're communicating with feels like they have the space to be vulnerable with you. Also, using phrases like "yes, please or no, thanks," and "help me understand this" are great ways to communicate kindness and willingness to have a productive conversation. Expressing empathy and having high emotional intelligence will make you a better communicator.

The Advantages of Good Communication

Effective communication provides you with an opportunity to build strong and valuable relationships with others. Whether you're in personal or professional settings, good communication is a skill that contributes significantly to less conflict and misunderstandings. It's important to know and understand the benefits of good communication because your approach to interactions will determine the quality of your relationships at home and in the workplace.

It Sets the Foundation for Strong Relationships

Good communication makes it easier for boundaries to be clearly defined during a conversation. When each person's limitations are put on the table, it allows for a safe, considerate, and respectful exchange of information to occur. Effective communication sets the foundation for strong relationships because it contributes to improving attitudes, creating closer connections, and facilitating personal growth. People are more likely to want to collaborate with you if they feel safe enough to share their perspectives with little to no possibility of backlash.

It Improves Problem-Solving Skills for Conflict Resolution

Another thing about good communication is that it improves your conflict resolution skills. Think about the listening process that we explored earlier in the book, that alone is an example of critical thinking. The core aspect of communication is attentive listening that promotes the engagement of higher-level thinking processes to allow for problem-solving to happen. To communicate effectively means to provide each person with an opportunity to listen and be heard. It enhances your capacity to see things from multiple perspectives and be more open-minded. Therefore, it equips you to develop more in-depth and valuable skills for conflict resolution. A combination of these abilities contributes to the advancement of empathy and awareness, thus making a conversation productive and pleasant.

It Boost Self-Awareness

Attentiveness and understanding are soft skills that are the heart of connection, and they allow you to develop your ability to look inward for clarity rather than seeking to blame others for things. Good communication helps you to see your side of the bubble in the way that things unfold around you. It provides you with an opportunity to introspect and be conscious of your feelings and emotions so that you can better address others'. By understanding yourself through self-awareness, you are more likely to notice your triggers before they turn into unhealthy behaviors.

It Cultivates Trust

Lastly, your ability to introspect will help you cultivate trust with people. Good communication isn't only an exchange of information but of the creation of trust as well. Your ability to be open and honest about your emotions or thoughts while giving others the space to do the same will make for good communication, which will strengthen the interpersonal bond between you and the person you are talking to. Also, the frequent exchange of trust between individuals allows them to draw closer to each other. To establish strong relationships, your communication needs to be effective, kind, and thoughtful. The next chapter will explore what communication in the workplace can look like.

Chapter 4:

What Is Communication in Professional Settings?

Communication is one of the most important skills you require for a successful life.
—Catherine Pulsifer

No matter the setting or environment, effective communication is held up by the same pillars, and works on the same principles. The communication that happens between yourself, an employer, clients, and colleagues is known as professional communication. It's a form of communication that uses a formal approach to exchanging information between groups of people. For example, professional communication happens when you give presentations at work or even send emails to your fellow co-workers about job-related topics. Anything that communicates information in your workplace, your job, or your career can be distinguished as communication that occurs in a formal environment or professional setting. This type of communication takes a structured approach to have dialogue which can manifest in any form of messaging starting from written emails to board meetings in person or virtual conversations. It's important to understand that formal communication, though direct and goal-driven, can be actually friendly. You can express your expectations and ideas to your team members in a kind and thoughtful way, in the same manner that you would if talking to a loved one.

Your communication in a workspace can range between fostering healthy and strong networking connections or missing out on great opportunities. That's why it's important to consider what your co-workers have to share. Good communication skills in a professional setting can help you to build strong and positive working relationships while avoiding misunderstandings and conflict. It's about embracing team differences and accepting that each person could have something valuable to add to a project, and everyone is an important part of the company's success. Friendliness in the workplace is less about formality or informality, but more about respecting the person that you're in a conversation with enough to consider your delivery when you communicate with them. Positive dialogue is important in interpersonal relationships as well as professional settings, and being able to communicate effectively with your co-workers will dictate the difference between success and failure in your business (Zenefits Team, 2022). When you can have a healthy communicative exchange with the people that you work with, it can encourage a constructive, happier, and more collaborative work culture which will inspire greater performance within the team and company in general.

Before the pandemic, much of the workspace communication happened in person. However, the way to conduct business has shifted to an online presence along with the face-to-face interactions since after the COVID-19 crisis. Many people now have the option of working from home and using virtual spaces more than physical areas to communicate with co-workers. Since formal communication has made a steady shift toward virtual avenues through applications (apps) such as Slack, Zoom, MS Teams, and Skype, people are no longer expected to share the same office to conduct business. Therefore, the professional landscape for communication has changed, which means that methods of how people interact must consider virtual forms alongside physical ones.

Workplace Communication Methods

Verbal communication is the one method of communication that we can use in the work environment, and it involves having a physical exchange of dialogue between yourself and colleagues. It's the use of words and body language to convey important information. For example, attending boardroom meetings or being in one office with team members and sharing information about work is a form of verbal communication. Considering the points mentioned in chapter three, verbal communication in the workplace also consists of empathetic and emotionally intelligent expressions. This means you shouldn't communicate with people without using these two pillars as your baseline. When you're articulating yourself in the office, it's important to also acknowledge what your colleagues have to say. For verbal communication to be successful, you must be willing to listen more than you speak. It means that you need to be open to teamwork which involves sharing your thoughts while attentively listening to others' ideas. A great place where you can practice this method is during presentations, when someone is sharing an idea, and you can take this as an opportunity to pay close attention to them and ask clarification questions afterwards. Assess their verbal and non-verbal cues and observe what they seem confident and unsure about. Once they've finished presenting and articulating their thoughts, then you can proceed to use the appropriate tone, words, and body language to respond—if a response is necessary.

Alternatively, written communication is a method that has gained popularity over time. Many employees and employers in workspaces use the written form of communication to exchange information. Written communication is mainly non-verbal, meaning that it also lacks body language and other non-verbal cues. As such, it can be easy to misinterpret tone and other valuable signals associated with the communication. So, it's important to learn effective ways to articulate yourself within the written communication workspace as well. Emails and other online (by using apps, for instance) correspondence make written communication methods. Some people might use emails to exchange information with co-workers while many people use virtual environments such as Slack or private platforms for communication. The use of effective and clear language is important when using the written language at work. You must use words and phrases that promote understanding and cooperation rather than being offensive to others. It's also important to state that your thoughts and opinions are yours and aren't meant to impose something on anyone else. For example, in a collaborative setting, you can share an idea and say something along the lines of "That's how I view this particular concept. Perhaps, other colleagues can contribute their valued input as well." Inviting other people to contribute to written communication opens the floor for everyone to feel valued and heard. Whereas, when you're using emails, you can use formal headings and sign-off such as "Dear [Whom it concerns]" and "Sincerely, [Your name]." Conducting yourself with eloquence when using written communication is essential because it greatly diminishes the possibility of misinterpretation and conflict. Always strive to be kind in your texts, even when you're reprimanding someone—do so with the intention to help them not belittle them. Also, choose short and concise messages to convey your idea on a forum because simplicity will help you minimize confusion. Using extravagant and fancy jargon to show yourself as professional or intelligent can derail the purpose of the conversation and leave co-workers confused rather than informed. Yet, choosing simple words that everyone can understand will increase comfort and improve trust between you and your colleagues.

Lastly, non-verbal communication in the workplace also refers to the use of tone, facial expressions, wording, and so forth. It encompasses all of the things that happen beyond our words and speeches. When you're thinking about non-verbal cues in the workplace environment, consider all the ways that you communicate without saying a word. What is your face saying? Is your tone sharp or gentle when you express yourself? If the words were muted, would your posture and delivery communicate confidence or uncertainty? Properly assessing what your non-verbal cues are communicating to your co-workers, can help your team accomplish its goals and reach success. Your gestures also add some understanding of what you're saying, so being attentive to how you express yourself will benefit you and your work immensely. Non-verbal and verbal communication cues are crucial to conveying an accurate message and intention for what you want people to know or even how you want them to feel in your interaction with them. Whether you're working from the office or from home, the two pillars and principles of communication still apply, and referring to the previous chapters can help you to communicate effectively in both physical and virtual workspaces.

Why Is Good Professional Communication Important?

Communicating yourself effectively is important in all settings because it's the best way to improve your connection with those around you. Good professional communication also builds trust between co-workers which helps to promote a supportive work culture that can lead to more enthusiasm and result in high performance. When people feel as though the communication channels are healthy and open, they feel accepted and encouraged to do their best on the job. A team that has effective ways of communicating with each other ensures that each individual is treated with respect, and that inspires more collaboration among them. People who feel happy and secure at their workplaces are more likely to want the company to flourish and grow. The way you communicate with your colleagues and associates also has the ability to attract more projects and network groups. Thus, good communication invites positive energy and success to any place. Knowing how to communicate at work can help you in many ways. You'll be able to ascertain which method of communication will work best depending on the situation. Some scenarios might require a quick email, while others might need a scheduled call or meeting to really drive the point home. Good workspace communication also ensures that everyone on the team is on the same page to properly execute responsibilities and get a great final product. Adequate communication is also important for a few more reasons. Let's explore them.

It's a Desirable Skill

Good communication puts you in a great position where employers are interested in your services and companies want to work with you. Having effective communication skills in the workplace sets you up for more opportunities that would otherwise pass you by. It will also make your job life a bit easier by reducing the chances of employee conflict and misunderstandings. Clear and effective communication is a skill that allows you to better interact with your co-workers, and also promotes a sense of belonging to the environment. Good communication helps you become a more approachable and involved co-worker, which means you're likely to increase your value within the workspace and make more friends.

It Improves Teamwork and Effort

Another great thing about being a good communicator at work is that you become a better team player. Good communication sets the foundation for productive and effortless workflow which improves the way you talk to and engage with your colleagues. Having a team spirit is a crucial aspect when you work in spaces that require engagement and interaction. You can't make a company or business succeed without effective communication and teamwork. Also, people with great communication skills are able to come up with brilliant ideas and products when they respect each other enough to listen and communicate effectively.

Whereas co-workers who aren't effective at communicating with each other will lack the motivation to collaborate, that will negatively affect the company's output. Low job satisfaction between colleagues and the workplace can make it difficult for people to engage with the work in front of them. Therefore, workers who are not satisfied at work, tend to find more reasons to take time off and are less productive than those enjoying their workplace (Martins, 2022). Good communication plays a crucial role in ensuring that all members of the company are satisfied with the work culture and stay productive with their projects in response to that satisfaction.

It Increase Productivity

Effective communication is a great motivator and tool for stress reduction. When people work in a healthy environment, communication should stay healthy to ensure employee productivity.

People need to feel valued and needed at the workplace, and when they are happy, it's easier to have a genuine desire to give more to work. Good communication makes people want to do more than the bare minimum to produce great results at work. In addition to that, good workplace communication saves time and resources by keeping teams on the same page to get the work done before the deadlines. People who communicate well spend less time trying to solve a conflict and have more time putting energy into executing the work as expected of them. Having good communication skills also helps leaders to delegate to their teams to promote constructive effort and enhance group performance. All of this makes showing up to work a lot more exciting for people. Because of effective and friendly interactions at work, there are less likely to be any conflicts.

It Minimizes Workplace Conflicts

When a task is communicated well, everyone involved in the project can get a shared understanding of what's expected, and each person can freely focus on their part of the job. Good communication reduces misinterpretation by promoting an environment for questions and clarification to flow between co-workers. In the workplace, miscommunication inevitably causes conflicts. So, effective communication helps to minimize this issue by guiding workers to focus on constructive collaboration and clearly deliver their ideas. When colleagues speak to each other respectfully and effectively, it also deters the creation of a hostile working environment; making employees happier. It also promotes a healthy work culture where the power dynamic between bosses and employees is maintained without a threat or tension. Workplaces that encourage safe and effective communication, and where everyone is respected and treated well, automatically motivates those involved to work smart and do even better than expected. It's also likely to keep people loyal to the company or business which builds the employer's reputation and saves time and resources for training new people.

It Encourages Loyalty and Collaboration

Employees are more likely to enjoy the work culture at companies with healthy communication, than those without it. People who are in a workplace that has a healthy collaboration culture and communication want to put their best foot forward because their creativity and ideas are encouraged rather than marginalized. Organizations grow stronger if good communication between all members is prioritized (Martins, 2022). More and more employees are likely to bring ideas forward to help the company to grow over time if good practices are valued and encouraged. Employee loyalty and collaboration generally come from people who have high job satisfaction. Otherwise, there would be no reason to remain at a place where you don't feel as though you have space to grow and can express yourself. People who stay at unconstructive jobs because they need an income are less likely to perform well or sing praises about the company if it doesn't have a healthy internal system. Good communication is integral to the success of any company and to the growth of its workers. If you're looking to communicate better within your workplace, the next section unpacks how you can go about doing so.

How to Improve Workplace Communication

Workplace interactions can influence your level of success in your career. When your interactions are productive and positive, they can help boost your esteem and confidence in the work that you do. However, when these interactions are negative, they normally result in stagnation and difficulty concentrating on the tasks that have been set out for you. Communication at work consists of sharing ideas, receiving, and giving feedback, as well as having project updates—all of which are methods of collaboration. The key to effective collaboration is knowing how to express yourself in the workplace (Martins, 2022). Being aware of how to properly talk to your colleagues in the workplace will make your job environment more fulfilling and satisfying. Below are some strategies you can use to begin improving your workplace communication.

Embrace Feedback

Feedback sessions should be a part of any work environment to allow employees and employers to check in and discuss project results, address ongoing issues, or share insights if something bothers either side. Workplace feedback helps establish a sense of continued understanding about the expectations for the job. When you are able to view feedback sessions more as an opportunity to learn and improve rather than view them as criticism, you'll begin to thrive in your work environment. You'll also begin to learn adaptive ways to communicate. Start embracing feedback from colleagues, clients, and employers as support and guidance toward self-improvement rather than feeling slighted when you've been given suggestions about your work or product. Embracing feedback as something positive is foundational to your personal growth. It will also help you become better at what you do. Try asking for feedback when none is freely given because there are always ways that you can improve, so don't let those pass you by. Depending on your job or what you do for a living, ask whoever is at the receiving end of your service for a review or feedback to help you get better at your craft for the next client or the next time you collaborate with someone. Embracing feedback also shows your willingness to learn and grow, which are great qualities to have in a work environment.

Show Willingness to Learn From Others

Effective workplace communication is a soft skill that makes you want to improve your abilities. When you're a good communicator, you get curious and ask questions about things that you don't understand, and by doing that you expand your existing knowledge. A person who thinks that they know everything never leaves room with any new knowledge. To learn new things to improve your performance at work, you need to allow others to teach you so that you can grow. If someone is better at something then you, don't get frustrated and try to outdo them, but instead ask them for a helping hand. Your willingness to allow someone else to teach you something new will help you see things from a fresh perspective. It will also upgrade your communication skills that will evolve together with your ability to perform at work. Even someone who isn't necessarily a "big shot" can teach you something, so go to work with an open mind and willingness to see what others can bring to the table and enrich your knowledge. Acting and responding to things as though you know it all can become a barrier to how much you're willing to learn. Moreover, it may negatively affect your approach toward communicating with others and your work performance.

Stay Engaged and Think Before Responding

Another reason why good communication in the workplace is important is that it keeps you engaged with the people around you and the work-related processes. You need to remain attentive to the environment you're in so that you can be a part of making it better. One way to stay engaged is by actively listening to what your colleagues have to say. Avoid dismissing or turning a cold shoulder to them just because you assume they have nothing valuable to add to a matter at hand. Consider the following questions: Why are you communicating? Who are you communicating with? What is the message you're trying to convey? What do you want the person to do in response? How can you best communicate to ensure that your goal is achieved? Train yourself to show up at work ready to listen without judgment or presumptions. That way you'll be prepared to absorb whatever knowledge is ready to lend itself to you. As you engage in conversations, make it a point to process the non-verbal cues such as the tone of voice from the speaker to see what they are communicating beyond their words. It will help you to be actively involved in the communication. Anyone can teach you something if you're willing to pay attention.

Make Things Simple

Finally, to improve your communication skills in the workplace you must be willing to keep things simple. I've mentioned this before: Stick to simple words and analogies that are easy to interpret and understand. There's no point in speaking all fancy for your co-workers, as your goal is to deliver the message and not lose the point along the way. For instance, when you're pitching ideas or have something to get off your chest be sure to keep it simple. Saying or adding too much fluff can complicate your message and dilute the information that you're communicating. This kind of message can easily cause confusion. Whether you're in physical or virtual work environments, it's important to be precise and cohesive with your information. The following section explores how to be an effective communicator in a virtual environment as in your physical workplace.

How to Effectively Communicate in Remote Workspaces

Seeing as remote workplaces require less physical interaction, they need a slightly unique approach for effective communication. Since the beginning of the pandemic, working from home has become increasingly popular. Whether people split their weekdays between the office and home or simply work from home, remote workspaces are a reality for many, and it can be helpful to be equipped with the tools that can make remote work effective and pleasant. The following tips can be used as a guide for how you can communicate efficiently and improve your workplace participation, even when you're working from your kitchen table.

Participate and Clarify Your Expectations

If there's one place where you can't afford to be unclear about your expectations and requirements at work is in a remote setting. Due to not seeing anyone's body language, you are more likely to misinterpret the tone of the written text than when you're communicating face-to-face. As a result, you have to be direct and upfront when communicating remotely, so that little to no room is available for misunderstandings. Clarifying your expectations can include reiterating what you want to get from the project in a bullet form. For example, "Hi, [Whom it concerns] these are the points that I would like for us to get through and get done by the end of this week [proceed to list bulleted points]." Clear communication in a remote space involves using many communication tools available to you to ensure that you get your point across without losing any essential meaning. Communicating your expectations also involves asking questions and leaving room for people to ask for clarification as well. Participation and communication within a work setting are the crucial aspects of a successful environment. It's important that you allow a flow of information to be exchanged between all parties. Allow yourself to interact with your colleagues through the use of communicative tools such as polls or ranking tools. You can't improve workplace communication by avoiding participation, so get involved and be a part of workrooms where you can uphold a relationship with other people on the job with you.

Restore Person-to-Person Communication

Participation involves showing up in virtual spaces that allow for an interactive dynamic to happen in the workspace. For example, if your workgroup arranges Zoom meetings and calls, be the first to confirm your attendance. You need to get proactive when working from home if you want to thrive in it. Restoring person-to-person communication in remote workplaces allows people to still feel as though they are part of a healthy and growing work community. If there's a lack of interaction at work (even virtual), it's easy for a team to feel lonely and isolated–a detrimental outcome to a company's progress. People need to feel connected and be a part of a greater purpose, and that can't happen without intentional arrangements to restore remote communication. Even though the work is happening online, people need to feel excited about working in the company. That's why it's important to get proactive and join work sessions with colleagues remotely. Even if it's not a work-related meeting! Otherwise, workers can quickly withdraw into their personal space and struggle to communicate themselves when called to do so.

Keep a Schedule and Focus on Performance

Another way to become an effective communicator in a remote setting is by creating a schedule for your projects. It will help you understand what your individual targets are and what you're expected to do on your end to benefit the whole team. Once you're clear and intentional about how you're going to work, putting in the effort and communicating what you need becomes more natural. It can be easy to lose interest when working in a remote space, so setting yourself time for focus and interacting with colleagues is crucial to help you stay determined. You've got to find a way to make things fun for yourself, even when you work from home. It will prompt you to continue to be effective and produce quality work. Good workplace interaction requires practice and patience, so challenge yourself to communicate with your co-workers as frequently as possible.

Engage in Casual Interactions in the Workplace

Your interactions don't always need to be formal and work-related. In fact, it's a great practice to have some casual interaction on your work platforms. For example, non-work slack or break channels can allow you to take a step back from the seriousness from time to time and connect with your colleagues. If your remote position doesn't offer this type of cool-down interaction, perhaps be the first one to suggest it. Casual interaction in the workplace can help you get to know your colleagues beyond work and can also build much-needed trust between yourself and them. These interactions are one way to strengthen your work community and improve your communication skills. Having an interactive, respectful, and open work culture where people can be more than employees or employers but can also be lay people, is great for business, for the culture, and for everyone involved. Some of the communication strategies that you've learned for your professional setting can be adopted in your home life as well. The next chapter will explore what communication can look like when it comes to personal life.

Chapter 5:

Communication in Personal Settings

Communication leads to community, that is, to understanding, intimacy and mutual valuing. —Rollo Reece May

When you communicate respectfully, clearly, and thoughtfully with others it will set a solid foundation for your relationships either at work or at home. Effective communication with your loved ones promotes feelings of safety and understanding that are needed for establishing strong connections. Opening yourself up to fostering healthy relationships involves expressing yourself wholeheartedly and honestly while maintaining consideration for other people's emotions. Your communication will touch the life of the person that you're speaking to, so do your best to be expressive without being nasty or unfair. If you aim to build relationships and not tear them down, then your words need to reflect that intention. Know that there are plenty of ways you can use to communicate yourself to others without causing a conflict. You also can train yourself in those ways. Your personal relationships are a huge part of who you are. Learning how to communicate and productively listen to your loved ones will help you improve your connections–together with your social interactions. This chapter explores personal relationships as well as the communication in them by unpacking how you can make your friends and loved ones feel heard and appreciated.

How to Make Your Friends and Loved One's Feel Safe During Conversations

The objective of any conversation should be to find common ground, feel heard and understood. If there are any issues, good communication should be carried out so that resolution and restoration of the issue can be possible. Communication is not about who's right. If you go into conversations with the intention to prove a point, then you cut the chances of moving forward in a constructive manner by half. Communicating well with your family and friends isn't about giving a lecture or showing who is the boss. It should be more about expressing yourself in a way that draws you closer together. As such, making your loved ones feel safe and valued during a conversation can go a long way. It's important to learn techniques for a healthy communication of your thoughts and beliefs. Making your loved ones feel secure in your conversations requires you to be vulnerable, compassionate, considerate, generous, and level-headed. Once these things form a part of your relationships, it gives the connection a better chance of succeeding.

Be Vulnerable: Share Your Emotions and Thoughts

When you're vulnerable you invite others to be open with you as well. It's the ability to mindfully invite others to your thoughts and emotions, instead of hiding them from people who care about you. As Mark Manson puts it, "Vulnerability is the key to better relationship" (Manson, n.d.). You can't build strong relationships if you aren't willing to be vulnerable with people, as it's the best way to connect with the world around you. Vulnerability is sustenance for any interpersonal relationship. It's essential for you to be able to connect on a sincere level with your friends and family or even a partner. If you want to have genuine relationships, you need to open your heart completely. That means being honest with them about what your boundaries are, how you feel, and what you need from the relationship. Being more vulnerable looks like being honest about your weaknesses. We can all improve on something, and vulnerability allows us to admit that to the people we care about. For instance, if you know that you could be a better listener, then being vulnerable would be expressing that message to your loved one. Working on yourself improves your relationships, and there's no shame in acknowledging where you could do better. Another way that you can practice vulnerability is by taking accountability for your emotions and actions rather than blaming others. Accountability can look like owning the outcome of things. For example, if you and your friend are having a fall out, being accountable would look like understanding that it's not all your friend's fault because there are some things that you could have probably done better to prevent the conflict. Taking responsibility for the things that happen in your life isn't an easy thing, it's far easier to point a finger at others. However, blame takes the power away from you and places it in the hands of the person to whom the finger is pointed. Acknowledging your mistakes can be empowering, and it's an understanding of your humanity—there's nothing more vulnerable than that.

Vulnerability can also look like showering your loved ones with appreciation every chance you get. We live in a world where it can be so easy to withdraw into ourselves after experiencing a breakup, but being vulnerable requires us to keep rising above failed relationships and continue to find ways to love strongly in new ones. If you want people in your personal life to feel your closeness, you'll need to share your emotions and thoughts with them. You can't suppress your needs or hide your emotions out of fear. People aren't mind readers, so it helps any relationship to progress when we are open and vulnerable with one another. Also, our vulnerability allows us to express self-compassion as well as show kindness to others.

Be Compassionate: Avoid Using Absolutes

Compassion is expressing kindness, especially during moments when it's difficult to do so (Jimenez, 2021). We show or share compassion with ourselves and the people in our lives based on the knowledge that we aren't perfect and sometimes we just need an extension of goodwill in our worst moments. Instead of putting each other down for our misfortunes, compassion allows us to respond with empathy and some level of understanding or willingness to understand. Examples of compassion include forgiveness, apologizing when your actions hurt others, knowing when to be sensitive to someone else, and being patient among other things. Expressions of compassion need to begin with the self to make it easier to empathize with others in their time of need. Using absolutes actually chips away at compassion, and it adds fuel to a difficult situation which can intensify feelings of frustration.

Absolutes can cause fractures in our personal relationships as these statements tend to discount the good that someone else does by overstating what they could improve on. For example, statements such as, "You *always* do this and that" or "You *never* make time for this and that" can be discouraging (Robbins, n.d.). Absolute statements are very often inaccurate representations of the truth. They generally serve to shut down communication or express frustration in an unconstructive manner, rather than concentrating on behaviors that one would like to see change. Avoid using absolutes by being completely clear about what's frustrating you, and instead of stating how your partner *never* helps with the dishes, address the issue by sharing how it would be helpful if he or she helped with the cleaning from time to time. Avoiding absolutes looks more like focusing on what needs to happen rather than keeping a record of how often it doesn't happen. Once you've set the use of absolutes to the side, you'll begin to see some positive responses to our needs, and your relationships will get stronger.

Another way to avoid the use of absolutes is by using "I" statements rather than "you" statements. Next time your partner or friend does something that upsets you or makes you feel strongly in some way, lean more towards expressing yourself by taking responsibility for your emotions rather than putting how you feel on them. For example, saying "I feel hurt when you walk away in the middle of a conversation" makes for a more productive dialogue than saying "There you go, always walking away when we speak" (Robbins, n.d.). By highlighting how something makes you feel rather than focusing on the behavior, you set the scene for a resolution to happen. Avoiding the use of absolutes is a way of showing compassion during frustrating situations. When you continuously practice showing up like this, it will build your emotional regulation skills and also help you form more resilient bonds with people. Then you'll be able to regulate your emotions by being more intentional when you speak. Even during moments of frustration, your attitude will convey that you consider how your actions will affect others—that's a wonderful way to ensure that your loved ones feel safe with you.

Be Considerate: Speak to Others How You Want to Be Spoken to

The act of being considerate refers to your ability to think about other people's feelings and needs through every step of the relationship (Gilbertson, 2016). It's about understanding that your actions, choices, and responses have the power to impact the experiences of others. So, when you think about that, you do your best to avoid causing harm to your loved ones. Being considerate includes avoiding the desire to be hurtful in the heat of the moment by doing your best to maintain mutual respect and understanding. For consideration to be at the forefront of your communication style, you need to learn how to distinguish between loving honesty and brutal honesty. Being harsh isn't equivalent to being honest; one helps to sustain the love in a relationship, even through difficulties, while the other damages the connection and taints the love.

When you are considerate of others, it promotes greater levels of affection and connection because it communicates your sense of thoughtfulness towards the people you care about. To be a considerate person is to think about how your behaviors and words will affect the people you love, and that makes you take time to process your emotions rather than impulsively act on them. When you consider how you impact others, you're likely to watch what you say and how you express yourself. For example, in an argument, you'll stop yourself from saying something out of anger because you know that it will cause deep emotional angst for the person on the receiving end. Consideration also encompasses the desire to understand perspectives that are different from your own.

Be Curious: Seek to Understand Another's Perspective

Curiosity is the active pursuit of new information, experiences, and understanding (Gross et al., 2020). When you are curious, you desire to know new things. In communication, it means giving the other person an opportunity to share their point of view with you. Being curious is about wanting to hear someone out, instead of forming your own assumptions about what they are thinking or experiencing. Avoid rushing or dismissing a person because you don't understand their true feelings. Instead, be curious and seek to understand them. Fight the urge to interrupt what the other person is saying and try not to react or make unnecessary comments when they are being vulnerable with you. Being curious involves listening to the speaker when they express themselves. You can't learn from being dismissive, you can only learn from paying attention to what's being communicated.

To cultivate curiosity and understanding in a relationship, you need to ask tough questions to get the answers you want (Smith, 2021). Learn to be straightforward about what confuses you and what you need to know, instead of being passive-aggressive. Stating what you need from a friend can look like saying, "What I need from you is patience" rather than reacting passively and tolerating that behavior. Whereas stating something like, "I'm a little confused by this, can you please help me understand what you mean by that" can also help establish a stronger connection and understanding between you and the person you are talking to. Part of being curious involves giving everyone in the conversation ample time to process and respond accordingly.

Be Generous: Allow Yourself and the Other Person Ample Time to Share

During communication, generosity will get you far. When you give people enough time and pause to process their feelings as well as what you've expressed, it helps you both find your way towards a resolution. Being generous with time, kindness, and consideration during communication is about listening without prejudice or hurry. Allow people to share what they have on their mind in a comfortable and safe space. Don't rush them to get to the point or undermine what they feel at the moment. Give them the time and respect to communicate their message, as you would want them to give to you. Perhaps, introduce an object that you can use to signify when it's each person's turn to share. For example, take a spoon from the kitchen and use that as an item to clarify whose turn it is to speak at a moment. If you're holding the spoon, it means that it's your turn to speak and the other person should listen. The talking spoon is especially necessary for individuals who have a hard time giving each other the grace needed to establish a connection and arrive at a resolution. These communication techniques require patience and level-headedness to accomplish a positive exchange of information.

Be Level-Headed: Being Overly Emotional Can Ruin Hinder Communication

Keeping your composure in frustrating situations is a self-management skill that allows you to separate your emotions from logic. You're better equipped to deal with conflict and frustration when you're level-headed in your approach to problem-solving. When you're communicating with your loved ones, it's crucial to maintain a sense of inner calmness to avoid lashing out and saying something that you might not actually mean. When you keep your emotions in check, it ensures that you can choose more constructive ways to communicate. Oftentimes, our emotions could lead us to do things that we wouldn't otherwise do if we took the time to process them before reacting. For example, if you're angry, it's better to step away for a few seconds rather than react explosively. Communicating from an emotional place can cause more harm than good to your relationships, as it can deter the intention of the conversation. The next section will guide you in how you can communicate with your loved ones and make them feel cherished.

How to Show Your Loved One's That You Appreciate Them

Appreciating people in your personal life is essential to helping you improve your communication skills. It's not always easy to share or be vulnerable with people, but we can teach ourselves to be comfortable with this over time. Learning how to communicate better with your loved ones is the first step towards showing your appreciation for them. The following tips should help you form an understanding of how you can go about expressing your appreciation to the people in your life. Doing this will grow and significantly benefit your relationships.

Check-In, Don't Check-Out

Sometimes it feels easier to walk away from conversations when they get too difficult, instead of working through them. Most of the time, taking a step back to cool down is the best decision. However, teach yourself not to stay away for too long even if you really need to step back, because it's better to manage conflict in relationships within the first 24 hours of an incident (Gulotta, 2022). Repairing an issue on the same day doesn't allow the incident to be more powerful and harmful than it needs to be. It means when the damage between you and the other person is addressed instantly, it offers you both a faster healing and the end of the problem. Confronting the issue should be approached in a way of checking in, but not in checking out that involves avoidance (when each person retreats to their own side and neither party wants to address the issue). Checking in requires each party to set their pride aside and communicate in a constructive way. Once you've both taken the time out to decompress, you can return to the conversation more prepared to overcome the problem with level-headedness. Confronting conflict within the first 24 hours also helps you to keep the warmth and love in the relationship, and it communicates that both of you are willing to work through the situation for the betterment of the relationship. Reparation and restoration of relationships are evidence of people who appreciate each other and are willing to put in the effort to work things out. It also conveys that you can make time, even under the most uncomfortable circumstances to show up for the people you love.

Nowadays we get so caught up in the hurry and responsibilities that we forget the importance of checking in on our friends and family. Being busy is not an excuse for not making time for your people. Be present with your loved ones because mindfulness and presence grow relationships. Spending quality time together strengthens relationships and offers you an opportunity to know one another on a deeper level. It also gives you time to gradually learn each other's communication styles. Checking in on loved ones also looks like doing small things to remind them that they're appreciated. For instance, asking about their day or wanting to know the simplest things about them will show them you care. Communication doesn't have to be serious all of the time, you can also have fun and use it to grow in the way you see others and how you see the world. You can never know another person enough, so truly be invested in checking in as often as you can.

Spend Quality Time With Your People

Plan dates and connection sessions with the people you care about. It doesn't matter how brief the encounters are, what matters is that you all make time to show up for each other. Spending quality time with your loved ones communicates that you're interested in getting to know them more, and you're interested in what they have to share. Spending time sharing activities together, doing things you enjoy. Quality time can bring joy to your relationships and draw you closer while helping you grow in empathy and care for each other more. It makes it more possible to extend grace in difficult situations.

Give Grace

No one is perfect, so be prepared to offer grace to the people you love when they fall short. Communication is about being emotionally intelligent and empathetic enough to understand that we won't always get it right. Sometimes we'll need to go over some things more than once before we can fully understand them. So, give grace to your people—it looks like forgiving the mistakes that they may make. Forgive so you can connect with others; don't hold grudges or hold things against people, the same way you wouldn't want that done to you. In the next section, we'll tackle social anxiety and the implications they can have on our ability to express ourselves.

Chapter 6:

Social Anxiety and Communication

That nervousness that makes your palms sweat and your heart race before you get up and make a speech in front of an audience? That's what I feel in a normal conversation at the dinner table. Or just thinking about having a conversation at the dinner table. —Jen Wilde

Social anxiety is marked by fear and avoidance of social situations (Cunic, n.d.). Also known as social phobia, social anxiety is a prolonged or overwhelming feeling of social encounters or situations. Many of us worry about external experiences but someone with social anxiety feels overly stressed and worried during and after a social situation occurs. Socially anxious people commonly experience persistent worry about being around people, so they avoid interactions in an attempt to shield themselves from possible humiliation, embarrassment, and misunderstandings. Experiences of social anxiety make it challenging to communicate clearly and confidently, and it can hinder a person's ability to form deep connections with others. Passive communication can be a sign of social anxiety—when someone uses indirect cues for communication rather than outrightly stating what they think or feel during a moment (Cunic, n.d.). Typically, people who use passive communication are too afraid to be confident in what they say, so they show signs of discomfort during a conversation. Though it may feel safe to communicate passively at first, it can increase feelings of anxiety and lead to resentment in the future.

The debilitating feeling of wanting to interact with others but being too afraid to do so can result in the manifestation of passive-aggressive behaviors such as manipulation, unclear expectations, and saying one thing and meaning something else, among other things (Gupta, n.d.). Passive aggression is usually a direct reaction to suppressing your emotions and the struggle to self-regulate, which happens over time if someone gives into their social anxiety. Though interacting with people may be incomprehensible or unmanageable, it's still the best practice to help you overcome social anxiety before it evolves into a clinical disorder. Communication is difficult enough without adding social anxiety into the mix, no doubt about that. However, many of us have experienced what it feels like to be socially anxious people and still have to push through the fear to connect with others. It's not an easy task. This chapter will explore what social anxiety is and how it can become a clinical diagnosis. We will also unpack how being socially anxious can influence your confidence in social situations.

Typical Manifestations of Social Anxiety

Social anxiety can manifest in a multitude of ways, and these vary from person to person. However, typical symptoms of social anxiety are characterized by fear-based responses that are either physical or psychological. Muscle tension and active fidgeting can be overt examples of physical manifestations, while overthinking and overanalyzing are innate examples of psychological manifestation. The typically experienced manifestations of social anxiety include momentary anxiousness about being judged by others and intrusive thoughts or overthinking (Abraham, n.d.).

The Fear of Judgment

Being afraid of what others think of you or what they'll think once you speak is a huge marker of anxiety in social situations. When you're fearful, you tend to support narratives that feed into that fear, and it makes it difficult to see outside of that bubble of thought. Social anxiety causes us to question others' intentions, and makes us doubt our own social skills, so we avoid interacting with people because of that. The fear of judgment that is linked to social anxiety can keep you from showing up to events and attending activities that matter to you. It can constrict your experience of joy in your life in a way that makes it hard for people to want to connect with you. Constantly feeling as though people will judge you for making an appearance or that you're bound to do something to embarrass yourself in front of others can hinder you from building a strong support system. Social anxiety is characterized by the fear of being judged and seen by others.

Intrusive Thoughts and Overthinking

When you're socially anxious, it's common to overthink everything; you think about what you're going to say, how you look, and how you're being perceived by others. The pattern of overthinking can make you not want to speak at all because you become increasingly afraid of making a poor impression on the people around you. Social anxiety can also make you lose track of the conversation as you become distracted by intrusive thoughts trying to convince you to find the negative in every situation. Having social anxiety and challenging yourself to be in public is undoubtedly one of the most difficult things to do. It makes it hard to decipher the truth from your fears, and it can keep you feeling overwhelmed enough to avoid people altogether. When you're overthinking, battling intrusive thoughts, and trying your best to appear one way in a social setting can make it hard to remain level-headed. All of this will affect your speaking abilities in anxiety-provoking situations, and it can hinder your chances to form positive connections. The implications of social anxiety on self-confidence and interpersonal relationships are massive.

The Implications of Social Anxiety on Relationships

Being anxious about social situations often makes it difficult to assess non-verbal cues without misinterpretation. It also makes it hard to start and continue conversations as well as to be assertive—all of which are integral to developing communication skills. It's more than shyness and experiencing social anxiety can cause distress and negatively impact our lives and relationships. Heightened anxiety causes low levels of trust during communication which makes it difficult to form genuine connections (Gardener, 2022). A relationship with no trust is likely to be unsatisfactory and cause unhappiness and a lack of support between the people involved. Social anxiety makes you want to avoid situations where you have to socialize, so it increases the possibility that you'll find more distanced ways of forming connections. For example, making online friends is likely the most comfortable alternative for someone with social anxiety because it offers the safety of getting to know people and being known without having to endure a person-to-person interaction. However, when you spend more time learning about people on the Internet, it's hard to tell if what they share with you is truthful. Remember, people can make up lies about themselves and be whoever they want to be on social media. So, you can never bet on whether you're building real connections online or not. Also, being removed from reality increases your chances to struggle to build strong relationships outside of the Internet—and that can worsen your social anxiety over time. Social anxiety can ease with age for some people, but for others, it won't go away without treatment. At that point it's usually classified as an anxiety disorder.

When Social Anxiety Becomes a Disorder

If social anxiety isn't well-managed, it can progress into social anxiety disorder which can be diagnosed and treated by a clinical professional or therapist. Social anxiety disorder (SAD) is the intense experience of anxiety that disrupts the ability of daily functioning (Cunic, n.d.). Gathering with large groups or meeting new people can emotionally destabilize someone with a social anxiety disorder to the point of having panic attacks. When social anxiety progresses to a clinical disorder, it makes it even harder to communicate with people or build new connections. Anxiety disorder can be categorized as the irrational fear of being watched, ostracized, or judged by others for being yourself—it can be debilitating. Unlike social anxiety, it can be difficult to talk yourself into going into public and overcoming the fear. Even if you get dressed and push yourself to go to a crowded area, SAD most likely will cause the feelings of fear to intensify. Whereas with social anxiety, these would probably subside after a conversation or two.

With SAD, no amount of proving that you're capable of managing an interaction helps the fear to subside at the moment you talk yourself to go to a public place.

Social anxiety disorder is caused by years of perpetual fear of social situations with little to no intervention, and it can also be a result of environmental and genetic factors (Cunic, n.d.). For example, a biological factor such as having an imbalance in brain chemistry can trigger symptoms of the disorder. When your brain has imbalanced amounts of serotonin, the hormone responsible for your emotions and mood, it can cause significant changes in your demeanor and lead to the development of SAD. Being overexposed to fear and increased anxiety over a prolonged period can also result in social anxiety disorder. Some of the external contributors to the development of SAD are extensive bullying, family conflict, and intense emotional trauma from overbearing or neglectful parenting (Cunic, n.d.).

Other physiological symptoms of SAD include trembling at the thought of interacting with others. It can manifest through excessive sweating, racing heart rate, and muscle tension. Alternatively, some behavioral symptoms could include avoidance, panicking in social interactions, and wanting to escape communicating with others. Many people struggle to maintain eye contact or initiate conversations because of SAD (Cunic, n.d.). Lastly, the cognitive symptoms may include unexplainable concern about how others view you, intrusive thoughts, and persistent dread of social interactions. If you suspect that you're experiencing social anxiety or may need to consult about the disorder–reach out to a psychologist or therapist for assistance. It is not a condition that you can self-diagnose and self-treat. If all you're experiencing are symptoms of anxiety about social situations, below are some self-help tools that you can use to challenge yourself to overcome that feeling.

Overcoming Social Anxiety—A Step Towards Better Communication

Your ability to feel confident and comfortable initiating conversations in various settings will help improve your communication skills as well as strengthen your relationships. However, social anxiety creates a barrier between you and the enriched life that you deserve to live. It causes unnecessary self-doubt, and it isolates you from building a community around you. Luckily, there are plenty of strategies that you can introduce as part of your daily routine to help you take small and controlled steps towards calming victory over your anxiety. It may take a while to build the confidence that you desire, but intentionally working towards it is something that will end up benefiting you in the long run.

You don't have to live a life of fear and self-doubt, and you certainly don't need to suffer at the mercy of your own thoughts. Learning how to cope with social anxiety requires confrontation, mindfulness, and self-monitoring. You need to be prepared to pay attention to your needs and fears so that you can actively address them and eventually go out into the world with confidence. Discovering effective ways to regulate your social anxiety won't only help you evolve as an individual, but it will be advantageous to your interpersonal relationships as well. People will begin to feel safer and better around a more confident and healed version of you. Experiencing anxiety can be discouraging, especially without the correct tools to assist you deal with it. The aim of this section is to empower you to help yourself when you feel overwhelmed by the thought of being in a social setting where you need to communicate with people. Social anxiety isn't a fun thing to experience, and perhaps learning some tricks on how to tame it can help you with future interactions.

Exercise, Eat, and Keep Healthy Habits

Physical activity and your daily diet are significant parts of your mental wellness. Taking care of your body and mind can build your confidence and lead to a more empowered version of yourself in public. If done regularly, setting aside some time to either take a walk, dance, or go to the gym can boost your self-esteem. It will make you feel good, energized, and perhaps more encouraged to communicate with others. Movement is a way to shake off tension caused by anxiety and burn your energy to promote positive feelings and sensations (Laderer, 2020). With a good diet and exercise routine, you can change mental barriers regarding communication, such as fatigue and anxiety, into focus. As you move, your mind also gains the clarity that it needs to establish deep attention to your thoughts through self-awareness.

Thought Journaling

It is an effective way to talk to yourself about how it feels to be socially anxious. Journaling is a self-awareness tool that allows you to safely evaluate your thoughts that may be overwhelming you during social situations. Consider the following prompts to guide you as you journal:

- What are some of the thoughts that go through your mind when in a social situation?

- How realistic is this thought?

- What would happen if you turned that thought in (by thinking the opposite thing) the next time you experience anxiety?

Journaling your thoughts will help you become more self-aware of your triggers and put you in a better position when it comes to processing and overcoming them. The aim isn't to judge your feelings and thoughts but to embrace and learn from them. Try to understand more about your anxiety, and use this understanding to help you break down challenging situations into smaller more manageable parts. Journaling can also lead to emotional, mental, and physical relaxation because it empowers you to purge yourself of all the negative emotions caused by stress.

Practice Exercises for Relaxation

Feelings of anxiety reduce the ability to feel at ease by causing symptoms such as a racing heart, faster breathing, and disorientation (Crinino, n.d.). Though fear is a common human reaction, it can stop us from having positive social experiences. Prolonged experiences of anxiety can limit the joy, happiness, and satisfaction that we can have in life, so learning how to manage these feelings is beneficial to us. Practicing relaxation exercises ensures that you actively enjoy activities that reduce symptoms of stress. If social anxiety is holding you back from building strong relationships and connecting with people, then the following activities should help you find relief and restore your confidence. When you practice how to relax, it pushes anxiety out of your life until it eventually doesn't overwhelm you and keep you away from forming healthy support systems.

Breathe Through It

Relaxation can be fostered through breathwork. Breathing has become so natural to us that we don't always realize how shallowly we use our breath. Learning how to breathe effectively is one significant way to start your journey toward becoming a good communicator by overcoming the anxiety that keeps you stuck. Actively breathing through anxiousness can support you through overwhelming feelings. When you're afraid, your body and mind react in a way to protect you from possible harm. So, breathing helps to reduce overactivity and keep you calm through the episode of stress. It can help you slow your beating heart and lower your blood pressure. Getting your breathing under control can be done in plenty of ways, but for now, you can use the following steps to get started:

1. Sit comfortably in a space that inspires calmness. Once you've found a quiet and safe space to practice your breathing, you can place one hand on your stomach and the other on your chest to assume the deep breathing position.

2. Inhale a slow and normal breath through your nose and notice the sensation as your chest and stomach respond. Use your hands to establish awareness of how this breath feels. As you inhale, the hand on your chest should remain in position, while the one on your stomach should begin to rise in response to your lungs expanding with air.

3. When your lungs have reached their capacity, you can slowly begin to exhale through your mouth. Thereafter, inhale again through your nose—while keeping the same position—and

exhale in the same way. Here, you can begin to channel deeper, more intentional breaths in and out through the nose. Remember to pay attention to how this motion feels and welcome the peace that comes with it.

4. You only improve through repetition, so continue this exercise as frequently as you need to. Eventually, you will feel easier to manage your anxiety by using your breath.

Practicing breathing makes it possible to stay mindful, which helps to combat any anxiety about the future. Being present takes your mind away from all the overthinking, and it brings you back to the current moment, where you can establish a sanctuary for yourself. Therefore, it helps to teach your mind to fight anxiety by remaining grounded and present at any given moment. Another meditative practice is visualization. It's effective in alleviating feelings of emotional unease and tension to help you become more aware of yourself.

Visualization

When you cultivate self-awareness, it helps you to develop the calmness needed to better communicate and express yourself to others. Visualization is about using your mind and imagination to benefit you. An anxious mind is usually filled with fear-provoking ideas, so visualization is a great strategy that you can use to silence negative thoughts and proactively instigate positive ones. The practice involves creating a mental image of a place that brings you the most peace and joy when you're in it to help your mind and body reach a state of relaxation. For example, if a sunny day by a quiet lake is a happy place for you, then visualization means envisioning it.

To practice visualization, you'll need to find a quiet place with no distractions where you can safely play around with your thoughts. You're allowed to create a place from your imagination if you can't think of anywhere realistic that brings you enough peace. When you find a quiet place around your home or office, sit comfortably or even lay back and relax. Make sure that your eyes are closed in preparation to visualize your happy place. Proceed to think about an ideal spot where you'd love to go to relax. While you're picturing that spot, think about the details that make it special. Envision the color of the sky on that day, and consider the aromas, sounds, and feelings of being in that place. Do your utmost best to create every single little thing the way you want it. As you create your place of peace, make sure to avoid complicating what you see and feel—keep the image simple enough for you to easily pull it out in moments of panic or anxiety. Then, imagine yourself physically experiencing the place that you've created. Think about what it would feel like to walk along the path there, and touch some of the objects in the vision. Keep your eyes gently closed as you enjoy the place you've created. Always draw on your breath as you concentrate on being present in the happy place and breathe to remind yourself to allow awareness to spread through your body. Whenever you're ready, you can inhale and exhale, before opening your eyes to continue with your day. If you ever need to go back to the mental image of the peaceful place, then do so without hesitation. It's okay to visit it as often as you get anxious, and it will help you to find calmness, and clarity, and ease your tension in real life.

Ease Muscle Tension

When we are anxious to attend social events, make speeches, or initiate conversations, it can cause physical tension to build up in our bodies. Sometimes, the best way to relieve that is to actively squeeze it out of the body through self-massages and movement. Experiences of anxiety require active relaxation strategies, which you can also do by relaxing your physical tension. To ease muscle tension during moments of stress, you can find a place where you feel comfortable, close your eyes, breathe with intention, and position your hands over the places of your body where it feels tense. For instance, start with one hand over the opposite shoulder and begin to massage the tension out of your shoulders—do the same on the other side. You can also use your hands to make tight fists as you actively visualize the stress leaving your body with each squeeze. Hold your fists closed, first gently and gradually growing tighter, until the count of 10. Also, while you either squeeze the tension or self-massage it out, remember to breathe through the movements. As you practice easing your muscles and squeezing out your anxiety, pay attention to the sensation you feel in the process. Continue to scan your body for tension and address any other areas that need self-massaging until you feel a significant reduction in physical stress.

Count Stress Away

Every relaxation strategy can be controlled by counting through movements and exercises. It is a quick and simple way to relieve feelings of anxiety. When you feel uneasy or overwhelmed, you can focus on breathing through your nose while counting to 10, 15, or 20. Depending on how long it takes for your lungs to fill up with air and release it, keep pushing yourself to higher counts to help you reach relaxation. The practice of counting takes your attention away from the stressful situation and makes you focus your energy on silently reaching your count. It encourages you to remain calm and present in anxiety-provoking situations. It's also a great instrument to use in uncomfortable crowds or situations that make you anxious. For example, you can make time to get a couple of counts in before you have to do an important speech. Counting trains your brain to slow down and focus during moments of stress, and it can help you develop a better outlook toward managing social situations.

Be Attentive to Your Mind/ Break Anxious Thought Cycles

Lastly, attentiveness and mindfulness are central themes in relaxation techniques. Anxiety is caused by thinking about future outcomes rather than focusing on the current moment, so practicing relaxation helps you remain present and reduce stress. Breaking anxious thought cycles in situations that require you to socialize is difficult if you don't pull yourself toward mindfulness. Being mindful is the mental state of being *here and now*. It allows you to see the value of the moment rather than be hard pressed about things that haven't happened yet—and may never happen. Remaining mindful permits your body and mind to rest in reality instead of racing elsewhere and creating anxious thoughts. To practice attentiveness and presence in anxiety-provoking situations, you can start by turning your attention away from the negative thought and towards your breathing. Once you are focusing on inhaling and exhaling, you can then shift your awareness towards your surroundings. Look at all the things that are happening outside of you and your feelings of stress. Be attentive to what you can hear, feel, see, and smell in your immediate environment. Also, if you can, identify what you can eat so that you can get your taste sense working as well. Create an inner dialogue with yourself where you comment on all of the things that you've become aware of. Check one thing at a time, explore the details, and describe what you want to mention about it. Play around with the idea of checking in with your feelings after observing each item pertaining to each sense. Making an exercise of shifting awareness from yourself to your surroundings and then back to yourself helps to make a bigger picture that doesn't put you at the center of everything. Therefore, this technique limits the likelihood of you feeling afraid of unlikely humiliation and embarrassment when you're around people.

Another way to break your cycle of anxious thoughts in a social situation is by playing along with the environment. For example, if you're at a party and a song that you know starts playing—sing along. You don't need to have a perfect pitch or know all of the lyrics, but permitting yourself to have fun helps you to come out of your shell. It will work in almost any setting and release your anxiety you might feel about approaching people for a conversation. It can also stop your mind from formulating unnecessary speculations about what people do and don't think about you.

Stop Assuming

Anxiety has a way of making us think that everyone is watching us, and we've bound to fail in front of them, but that's far from the truth. Everyone is so busy thinking about themselves that they don't have time to think about us. The sooner we learn to stop jumping to conclusions in social settings, the more at ease we'll begin to feel in communication with others. Instead of pulling up speculations, rather take things for what they are and read people for what they are showing you. In other words, be present and ask questions about things you're curious about. Now that you're equipped with some simple and helpful techniques to ease your social anxiety in public situations, you may find the next set of daily strategies for communication helpful for initiating conversations.

Chapter 7:

Daily Techniques for Effective Communication

Communication is a part of everyday life, and it's a skill that can be useful for all interactions. When we can use communication to establish safe and trustworthy connections with others, our lives start to flourish. By using those skills, we discover how to overcome conflict and find resolution in relationships. Effective communication strategies help us to grow as individuals, thus making us better people to interact with. From a constructive standpoint, disagreements in relationships are easier to understand and work through when the people involved in the conversation know the tools to communicate constructively. Learning communication techniques also prepares you to diffuse situations that may lead to unprogressive conversations. This in turn, helps to strengthen your relationships in the long run. Knowing how to communicate effectively also helps you to know when to stop talking and give room for a dialogue to happen.

Effective communication makes interactions and exchange of information with others more enjoyable. Even so, we don't always know how to begin communicating in a way that's beneficial to us and the relationships that we intend to foster. So, this chapter sets the foundation for effective communication by providing daily techniques you can use to either manage social anxiety or overcome ineffective communication.

Why Bother Communicating Effectively?

No one wants to live alone. Having a community or a support system helps us to get through life in a healthier and more productive way. We can't establish lifetime relationships if we aren't willing to communicate effectively. The only way for someone to learn about you and for you to learn about them is through communication. Your home and work relationships depend on how well you're able to express yourself while listening to other people. You can't have healthy and happy connections if your communication style is ineffective. It can also hinder intimacy and trust in relationships which can leave you feeling isolated and lonely in the world. Having effective communication or learning how to improve your approach to communication is integral to developing your partnerships and interactions. If you want to have beautiful and encouraging connections with people, you must be willing to dig deep and discover ways to communicate well. The significance of proper and effective communication has already been unpacked in the previous chapters. This section, however, aims to give practical communication strategies that you can implement in your day-to-day life. Having quality conversations allows you to establish quality connections. You can use the following strategies to form the basis for how you communicate with others.

Communication Techniques for You

Most of the anxiety you feel about interacting with others is determined by your outlook toward communication. Too often, we believe that communicating is about how we appear to others, what we say, and what we do. Yet, communication is more about giving the other person the space they require to express themselves to us while being in a safe and non-judgmental environment. In that sense, communication is more about listening and paying attention to what someone else has to share, and feelings of anxiousness are likely to overwhelm us when we lose sight of that. Imagine going into a board meeting or having an interaction with a stranger. Your mission is to learn more about them than you are to share about yourself. This mind trick will then make you feel less anxious about initiating a conversation. Communication is supposed to be an exchange of information that's centered around what the other person has to give, rather than putting pressure on us to speak our heads off. Next time you go and interact with someone, make it about them. Be curious to see what you can learn from simply listening, asking questions, and being attentive to them. When you can learn how to be effective in your communication, you will start to feel overcoming that feeling of anxiety, and you're less likely to overthink a potential interaction.

Communication is much simpler than we give it credit for. Learning to make it more about what we can hear, see, and learn, teaches us to sharpen our humility and empathy toward others. Our daily interactions should be more about what we don't know rather than constantly trying to prove what we know. The act of communicating is made more challenging by the need to impress or come across as an intelligent person. However, when we can sit back and let the conversation shape up to benefit all those involved, life becomes easier. Everyone can be interesting when they're given the chance to speak and be heard. So, make it a mission to do that in your interactions. Be the person who listens and actually hears what someone else has to share instead of the one who interrupts or feels the need to make the moment about themselves. The more pressure you take off yourself, the less frightening your interactions will become, and the better your relationships will start to feel.

Nevertheless, communicating can feel challenging if you don't know how to show up effectively. When you lack the necessary tools and techniques to manage a good conversation, it leaves room for misinterpretation and conflict. Improving your communication skills can improve your entire life because forming good connections is at the heart of living a good life. Though your happiness is your responsibility, creating a great support structure through effective communication can increase feelings of joy and belonging in life. Learning valuable communication techniques is integral to your relationships, and also the way you end up experiencing life. You're more likely to enjoy your life when you know how to deliver information effectively. The communication techniques that will be covered in this section are clarity, proactive listening, attention to detail, use of empathy, giving and receiving feedback, and validation. With these techniques, your communication style will attract and invite people to connect with you rather than push them away. When equipping yourself with the necessary techniques for communication, it makes life better by reducing the pressure and anxiety that comes with interacting with people.

Be Clear

Self-awareness forms a massive part of how you communicate. You can only express yourself clearly when you are in tune with what you need and want to get from the moment. Confusion in communication usually happens when people aren't attuned to their thoughts and emotions, since you can't communicate what you haven't even taken the time to understand. Your ability to improve your knowledge will make it easier for you to be clear when you talk to others. For example, if you know that you aren't a late-night person, you won't feel guilty about expressing that you prefer meeting for breakfast with a group of friends or colleagues. Good communication occurs when you are fully aware of your boundaries, strengths, and weaknesses.

Being clear during conversations involves sharing information, and doing so in such a way that doesn't create confusion. It's important to be straightforward in interactions with others and to allow them to be upfront with you too. You can create confusion when you try to express your true thoughts and feelings during a conversation by going out and about. So, it's better to just be forthcoming. It includes saying what you need with confidence rather than shying away in fear of the outcome. Being clear in communication also involves not mumbling your words when you speak—be direct and audible. Speaking with clarity helps the receiver to get the idea of where you're coming from, thus limiting the chances of misinterpretation and confusion.

Practice Proactive Listening and Responsiveness

Listening is the greatest responsibility of someone who's a good communicator. Intentionally paying attention to the speaker can guide your response objectives and make for a wholesome conversation. The nature of communication is to have an expressive dialogue, and you can only do this when you're self-aware but also attentive to what the other person is communicating (that includes interpreting nonverbal cues). Active listening shows the speaker that you're interested in sharing the moment with them. You can practice proactive listening through the effective use of gestures, asking good questions, giving feedback, and reflecting on the dialogue through respectful and appropriate body language and expressions. Make the other person feel appreciated by keeping your focus on them and their message.

Also, be responsive to what others are asking because it shows them that you value their thoughts. Responsiveness in appropriate pockets of the conversation is a great way to show the speaker that they aren't alone in this communication. Responding to their queries and concerns, or even their ideas, instead of ignoring or dismissing them, is a part of active listening. You can do this by nodding first to show that you're present in the conversation and then addressing the topic if necessary. Alternatively, to show that you're listening, you can maintain eye contact and avoid fidgeting while the speaker is sharing information.

Be Attentive to Non-Verbal Cues

People say a lot in what they don't say. Being attentive to someone else's nonverbal cues, such as facial expressions, body gestures, and movements, is a great tool for communication. It can help you address things that otherwise would have been ignored. For example, you can pay attention to someone's face when you're sharing information to gauge their thoughts about the topic. If someone's eyes go wide and their facials embolden in shock, it can be an opportunity to address the reaction in the moment by stating, "I noticed that you reacted in XYZ to this information. Is there something you'd like to add or that I've missed?" Paying attention to nonverbal communication is beneficial to any conversation because it gives more insight into the thoughts and feelings of the listener and the speaker alike. It also sets the scene for empathetic moments to originate more naturally.

Extend Empathy

As you know, empathy and emotional intelligence uphold the structure of communication. Without these pillars, there's no progress in communication, and there's a chance for a massive conflict. Extending empathy to people during a conversation involves making provisions for what they may not know. We are all learning and trying to grow, so being empathetic is almost an acknowledgment that we're all flawed and deserving of compassion. In moments of conflict, empathy can help us avoid the urge to respond aggressively. It makes us keep our composure in frustrating situations, thus allowing us to process information a bit better before responding. Practicing empathy can look like taking 10 seconds to cool off before addressing a situation that upsets you. Giving yourself time to process also provides you with the space to respond from a considerate and empathetic standpoint. An empathetic conversation is constructive because it focuses on connecting rather than being right, which makes us open to feedback.

Be Open to Receiving and Giving Feedback

It's easy to get caught up in the moment or how something makes you feel and interpret helpful feedback in a negative way. Sometimes, hearing that you can improve at something makes it hard to be confident in your capabilities, but feedback helps us become better. For example, when your boss or colleagues express things that you can improve on, it's good to see this as a learning opportunity. Rather than reacting to what someone says without fully understanding what they mean, always ask for clarity, and implement the changes required to help you improve. Also, asking for feedback requires you to be humble enough to ask people how well they think you're doing and if you've improved from the last time they pointed out something about you.

Validate

Another technique that you can use to become an effective communicator is validation. Be attentive to the emotions, thoughts, and suggestions that other people give and make it a point to validate them. Validation involves respect and acceptance of different viewpoints and embracing the truth that you can learn from others. In communication, it's important to show a person that you're listening to them, even if you don't agree with their position. Validation allows you to support the perspective of another without having to conform to it. Multiple statements that you can use to show someone validation include:

- "I can see how you would feel this way."

- "I hear how frustrating it can be."

- "I'm here for you."

- "I feel the same way."

Whereas invalidating statements can make someone feel as though their feelings and thoughts aren't important. Invalidation can leave an emotional scar on people by taking away from their experiences and right to express their emotions. Some of the phrases that show invalidation can include:

- "I don't want to hear it."

- "You should feel lucky."

- "I think you're being too sensitive."

- "If you hadn't said that I wouldn't have responded hurtfully."

Invalidation can be harmful to relationships and cause a fracture in emotional connections with others. When people feel validated, it makes them feel safe to express themselves and share their opinions without fear of being judged (Salters, n.d.). By using the techniques mentioned above, you can improve your communication skills and help yourself foster effective interactions daily. The next section explores the multiple self-monitoring techniques that you can combine with the skills you've already learned to help you navigate everyday communication.

How to Improve Everyday Communication

Building on the techniques listed in the previous section, improving daily communication also includes exposing yourself to social situations instead of avoiding them. Paying attention to your tone when you speak, and improving your emotional intelligence will do wonders. We touched on the latter in chapter three under the section *How to improve your empathy and emotional intelligence.* Check back on that information and allow it to set the basis for this section as well. Improving daily communication takes practice and intentions, and you can't become better at something if you aren't determined to constantly work on it. This means you need to create opportunities to communicate with people every day. You should challenge yourself to at least speak to two or more people daily about a range of topics. When you continuously put yourself in positions where you need to interact or face your fear of communicating, you begin to empower yourself.

It's much like exercising, to become fit you need to commit to hitting the gym often. Ultimately, you become better at communicating because you keep on facing the mountain of communication on a regular basis. Communication isn't just a one-and-done thing; it requires you to commit to actively shaping your skills in every conversation for the rest of your life. So, make it exciting by setting yourself daily or weekly goals for the minimum conversations required and how often you need to interact with new people. Also, monitor yourself in every interaction through the practice of awareness. Be intentional about noticing some of the things that you can improve on from conversation to conversation and allow yourself the room to develop. The points below can be used as a guide to help you take small steps toward improving.

Create Chances for Communication by Limiting Your Avoidance

Avoiding social situations and having conversations with people won't help you become an effective communicator. You need to encourage yourself to overcome moments of temporary discomfort in an attempt to improve your communication skills. Allow yourself to face what makes you feel afraid because when you do that, you can ultimately overcome it. Putting yourself in positions where you need to interact with others will help to boost your confidence and self-esteem over time. When you limit your avoidance of social situations, you subconsciously reprogram your mind to believe that you're capable of conquering social interactions. Therefore, you'll start to feel less afraid of being assertive in public, and you'll find yourself getting more comfortable with the idea of initiating a conversation. A couple of ways that you can begin to assert yourself are by hanging out with people, starting, or contributing to healthy debates, and asking people questions. To be a good communicator you must put yourself in positions that exercise your communication skills so that they can become refined. If going to social events is a huge step, you can start small by communicating with people at home instead of being locked in your office or room until the next morning. You can also call a friend instead of texting them. This way, you are forced to carry out a dialogue and engage in a beneficial way. Communication also hinges on your tone of voice and willingness to contribute to the conversation.

Consider Your Tone

The tone of your voice is a significant part of any conversation. You could have the best intentions for someone, but if your tone toward them was harsh, then your intentions won't come across the way you'd like them to. Your tone involves how you say something rather than what you're saying. For instance, if you're shouting something to someone in an aggressive way, it's likely to communicate frustration instead of excitement. How you say things is just as valuable in communication as what you say. Practicing your delivery beforehand isn't a bad idea. If you know that you have an important or upsetting conversation coming up, take the time to practice how you'll say things. A harsh tone is a breeding ground for stagnation in conversation, and especially for miscommunication.

Practice Emotional Intelligence

Going back to the third chapter, emotional intelligence is all about being self-aware, regulated, motivated, and having good social skills. To practice developing these things, you need to get comfortable with problem-solving, taking accountability for your mistakes, engaging with different people, and actively listening. Basically, practicing emotional intelligence is about honing all the skills that have been discussed in the book so far. It's almost impossible to have a good read of a conversation if your emotional intelligence is low and unestablished. Now that you've received the tools you need to evolve your daily communication, the final chapter is about using what you know to build strong relationships: It all starts with you.

Chapter 8:

How Self-Care Can Help You Communicate and Build Stronger Connections

Accept yourself, love yourself, and keep moving forward. If you want to fly, you have to give up what weighs you down. —Roy T. Bennett

Most of this book focuses on how you can establish strong relationships with people in your life by using effective communication strategies. Much of building a community involves focusing on the impact you have on other people's lives. However, your external footprint has to begin with the energy that you have and give toward yourself. Communicating and interacting with others is always going to be an extension of your relationship with yourself, and that's why shaping your self-image and fostering intrinsic confidence is important. When you aren't caring or loving yourself properly, you will struggle to care for and love other people, too. Therefore, no matter how much you learn the tools and tricks for effective communication, you'll struggle to implement them in your life if you don't have the sense of self-respect and awareness which comes with caring for yourself.

To establish healthy connections and build rapport with others–you need to embrace yourself wholeheartedly. Relationships and communication thrive when the people involved know who they are and can be authentic in the way they relate to others. Trying to learn people before you even have an understanding of yourself, and your needs can be detrimental to fostering strong relationships. When you don't care for yourself, there's no way of fully expressing what you desire to make a relationship work for you. Therefore, it gives manipulative people a chance to overstep, and it pushes genuine people away because they begin to see that if you can't fight for yourself, then you could never stand up for them either. Also, not caring for yourself leaves you vulnerable to violating other people's boundaries. When you aren't self-aware, you can put yourself in positions where you disrespect other people's needs and desires. It can also make it hard for you to accept it when people make decisions that are best for them, even if those choices don't reflect what you want. Not having a healthy self-relationship can hinder your ability to express affection and warmth to other people because you can't give what you don't understand. The techniques and knowledge provided in this book so far can help you build strong relationships. Even so, the best way to build good interpersonal relationships with others is by having a healthy way of relating with yourself. In this chapter, you will learn practical ways to become a better version of yourself so that you can use all the tools provided in this book, to effectively communicate and build rapport with those around you. Listening, validating, and connecting starts with you.

Start With Self-Care

In chapter six, we touched on exercising, eating well, and forming healthy habits to combat social anxiety—these are all forms of self-care. The health of your relationships and the success of your connections begins with how you treat yourself and how much effort you put towards improving your connection with yourself. Building strong relationships isn't possible without having a good internal dialogue. Everything that happens around you begins within you. The way you respond to and communicate with others is largely affected by the parts of you that are healed or are still in the process of healing. People who don't have a healthy relationship with themselves often have a toxic approach to communicating with others. Typically, it's the one that tends to lack empathy and emotional intelligence. By creating a positive way of relating with yourself, you indirectly build a foundation for how you're going to relate with the environment around you. If there's no peace within, then you're likely to experience a noticeable amount of chaos in the external world.

Self-care is one of the most overlooked yet most fundamental ways to make the world a better place. It can significantly transform your quality of life, relationships, and work. Caring for yourself is essentially actively prioritizing the relationship that you have with yourself and strengthening the self-connection. When you prioritize yourself, it enables you to have a rich experience of other relationships and of your life. It offers you more joy, authenticity, and better mental and physical health. Self-care helps you to understand your emotional triggers so that you can better regulate them. It also makes it so you can have a more optimistic outlook of dire circumstances and interpret events more objectively throughout your life. As you learn to become more patient, vulnerable, committed, and trusting of yourself, you will be able to transfer those same qualities into the relationships that you have with others. Self-care is a way to make you a happier, more vibrant, healthier, and more productive person. That's why this should be a necessity rather than something that you push to the side or do out of convenience. Caring for yourself will help you foster mindfulness for others, that's why self-care isn't selfish. It's a way of showing up in a positive manner for yourself and the communities around you.

Self-Awareness Begins When You Communicate Yourself to You

To put it simply, self-awareness is knowing yourself by understanding your emotions, thoughts, strengths, and limitations. Taking the time to appreciate yourself and build who you are can help to establish better ways to communicate and express yourself to others. Self-awareness is a journey that consists of understanding and remaining true to yourself and your beliefs (Murphy, 2017). It's based on your ability to be introspective throughout your life and fostering conscious living in the process. Try practicing the following things to establish self-awareness:

Spend Time on Your Own

Before you can truly enjoy anyone else's company, you need to be satisfied and content on your own. Spending time alone can be empowering if you allow it to be, as it gives you a chance to really pay attention to your emotions and thoughts without being distracted by the world around you. Being just by yourself is an opportunity to foster self-trust and knowledge. When you spend time on your own, you get to improve your mindset by noticing your negative thoughts and working to transform them. You can view spending "me time" as a way of checking in on your emotions and feelings, as well as realizing your perspectives and beliefs. As you're always growing and changing, time alone gives you a chance to stop and be attentive to where you are so that you can build toward where you want to be. Fostering self-awareness by spending time alone can help you understand the underlying ideas and cognitive processes that influence your mood and feelings. You can ask yourself some questions and journal your answers to help you get the most from solitude. These can include: "What am I feeling right now?", "What do I need today or even this week?" and "In what ways do I need healing?" Sitting with yourself and being able to ask yourself *what questions*, instead of *why questions* can help you get to the root of the person you are as well as understand what things affect you and in what ways (Murphy, 2017). Spending time with yourself ensures that you can get started on your journey toward self-discovery. The more you uncover about yourself, the better your interactions with others will become.

Do Things to Support Yourself

The more you show yourself that you're in your corner, the better your experience of your life will be. Self-care looks like setting up a healthy routine and speaking to yourself in affirming ways. It's also about recognizing that you aren't your thoughts or feelings. Instead, you're the person experiencing them—that way, you can observe your emotions rather than identifying with them. For example, you'll acknowledge sadness as the way you *feel* rather than who you are. So, you'll say things like "I am *feeling* sad" instead of "I *am* sad." Doing things to care for yourself is a very broad method that involves physical exercise and noticing your mental processes at any given time. Once you start executing things that show you support yourself, you will gradually begin to notice how you improve in supporting others.

Listen to Your People More Often

You can grow from learning how others view you. Listening to your people encompasses your willingness and ability to hear who your loved ones say you are and how they feel around you. These observations and evaluations can be added to your awareness of self. Knowing yourself isn't just about tapping into your inner knowledge but also about permitting yourself to hear from those you care about when they tell you how you can improve. Hearing what people say about you, gives you the opportunity to work through some of the blind spots that you may have. And to do so, you need to eliminate self-condemning. Listening to your people isn't about finding reasons why you should love who you are but more about understanding how people perceive you so that you can learn more about yourself. Now, if you hear something that you don't agree with or that you don't like–try not to internalize it. Instead, use that information to confirm with others whether they perceive you in the same way or not. Often people's perceptions can be influenced by their own biases, insecurities, and fears, so it's better to check statements across different aspects of your life. It means, don't just take the word of one friend, ask around. Think of your self-discovery journey as a research project–you need as much feedback from different people to truly speak of who you are.

Own Your Thoughts

Listening to the people you care about isn't the only way to learn more about yourself. You can also learn by listening to yourself. What are your thoughts telling you about how you think and process the world? How can your thoughts help you improve moving forward? Owning your thoughts looks like embracing what they are by way of observation rather than judgment. Your way of thinking speaks a lot to what you've grown to believe about yourself, and what you think about the world. So, give yourself a chance to let your thoughts guide you toward understanding your fears, desires, and goals in life. Once you feel empowered enough to own your thoughts, you can begin to establish new and positive patterns of thinking. Remember, self-awareness is anchored to self-love. At no point in this journey should you attack, marginalize, deny, or harm yourself. Instead, be open and willing to learn—that's how you'll grow. Getting through this journey will require patience and establishing healthy boundaries. The latter will be explored next.

Establish Healthy Boundaries

Boundary setting is a great form of self-care, as it helps you protect yourself from low standards while still letting people in and forming genuine connections. Healthy boundaries aren't walls meant to keep people out, but they are doors that are supposed to let good things in and keep bad influences out. You can have boundaries at home and at work, and establishing these can help you express yourself better to people. Boundaries are a way of communicating what you will and won't accept from yourself and others, whether it's the treatment you receive or the way you're spoken to. Research suggests that setting healthy and flexible boundaries can improve wellness, self-control, and communication skills (Brooten-Brooks, 2022). Boundaries can be classified under three distinguished categories: flexible, rigid, and open. Flexible boundaries are known as clearly expressed boundaries that can be adapted depending on the situation. These boundaries are associated with the types of rules we set for our loved ones, such as family and friends. Flexible boundaries are connected to support and warmth, but at the same time, they allow you to have the control and assertiveness necessary to stand by them because they offer stability. Whereas rigid boundaries are the opposite—these are inflexible and closed off. When you set this type of a boundary, it means that you hardly allow anything into your space or your life. Rigid boundaries make it difficult for people to engage and interact with others in a healthy and effective way. A person who has firm rules is likely to be more withdrawn and isolated in their lives compared to those with flexible boundaries. Alternatively, open boundaries are too loose and unclear to the point of confusion and frustration. People with open boundaries are more likely to struggle with their needs being met because these are so loose and hard to explain. Loose boundaries can be a massive sign of a codependent person.

The best type of a boundary that you can set for yourself is a flexible and clear one because it helps you communicate what you need with confidence while leaving sufficient room for you to change your mind as you get older and more mature. Healthy boundaries are the type that invites people in but show them the door when they overstep. A healthy boundary empowers you to stand by your rights and advocate for yourself and your needs. These ensure you are protected emotionally, physically, sexually, and otherwise. Clear boundaries are also about honoring the needs that other people may have and respecting their limitations. Establishing healthy boundaries is a great way to initiate a state of happiness and peace in your life.

How to Set Clear Boundaries

Setting healthy boundaries begins with being self-aware. To get clear with others about what you accept and don't accept in a relationship, you need to know yourself fairly well. It's easier to lay down rules for yourself and others when you are clear with yourself about your expectations. Also, establishing a good communication style will help you express yourself more assertively and with clarity (Nash, 2018). Being assertive means being confident in expressing your boundaries openly and respectfully. It also helps you to remain sure about what you want, even when people try to sway you otherwise. To set healthy boundaries, you'll need to use the next steps as a guide:

1. Be as straightforward as you can about what you expect without shouting, being harsh, or unkind.

2. Be direct about your needs, rather than focusing on what you don't like about something or what you don't like. Ensure that your communication focuses on what you expect, instead of causing confusion by communicating the opposite.

3. Be comfortable with the discomfort that will arise every time you express your boundaries to people. It may feel weird and not fun to share your expectations, but stand by them without guilt or judgment, there's no shame in protecting yourself and your space.

Hopefully, these three steps can help you discover more effective ways to express your own boundaries to people. Be sure to stand by your word because how you reinforce and respect your own barriers will inform how others do the same. Examples of clear boundaries include stating how much time you have to do lunch with a friend to let them know that you expect your time to be valued. Or declining an invitation to something that you aren't interested in attending. The first example can be supported in the following scenario: Imagine your friend asks you to go for lunch with them, for what's supposed to be a quick catch-up. You tell them that you only have two hours to spare for lunch, so they need to be on time. Nonetheless, despite your clear position, your friend arrives an hour later—with boundaries, you're allowed to spend the time left of those two hours with them and leave once it's over. It's not your job to shuffle your boundaries for people who don't respect them. Sure, your friend might be disappointed that you won't give them more time, but you have nothing to feel guilty about once you've expressed your clear boundary to them. Boundaries give people a chance to show up for you in ways that you need them to, they also give you an opportunity to extend the same respect.

Get Restful Sleep

Setting time aside for your mind and body to rest is also a way to establish a boundary. Restful sleep helps you to relieve stress which gives you more energy and mental capacity to interact in your relationships and participate in self-care activities. Sleep is important for optimal brain functioning, and getting enough rest will help you to stay focused and productive throughout the day. It will also make it easier for you to have the energy and level-headedness necessary to express yourself effectively when you communicate with others. Another stress relief strategy is meditation.

Start Meditating

Meditating allows you to relieve short-term anxiety and establish long-term health. It involves fostering a sense of internal peace by using your breath, affirmations, and mindfulness. Meditation is all about finding stability in the present moment and being able to relax into the experiences that are happening for you at the moment without paying attention to anything else. You can meditate while sitting or even while walking, either one is fine as long as you're exercising a deep sense of presence. To practice meditation, you need to first focus on your breathing—use the same deep breaths that you learned in chapter six. Do this by placing your hand over your stomach and feeling the sensation of your breath through the expansion of your lungs as they press against your belly. Once your breathing is in check, you can slowly begin to meditate. If you choose walking meditation, the point of it is to pay attention to every step you take. Acknowledge and absorb the scenery as you walk from one place to another without rushing. Whether you're on a work break or have the luxury of time, take every little detail in about what you feel and what you see around you. Allow the walk to refresh your body and your mind as you take in the crisp air, the scents, sounds, and colors around you. Take it easy and cherish each moment.

The same sentiment works for sitting meditation. You can practice it by finding a quiet and comfortable spot to take in your emotions and thoughts with ease. As you allow yourself the experience of sitting and processing your presence, avoid the urge to judge or rush the moment. Let your breath be your point of focus, and you can even close your eyes if you need to. Meditation is supposed to help you tune in all the wonderful sensations that you may miss on a busy day filled with responsibilities. It's your moment to take claim of your body, space, and needs. During meditation, your mind may wander into its own thoughts and imagination—that's normal, let it do so. Typically, as your mind relaxes, it's likely to roam into different thoughts and ideas. It's okay to permit your imagination to wander as your thoughts begin to move into daydreams. You're allowed to experience that moment of belonging without judgment or trying to control it. If your mind wanders during meditation, simply permit yourself to take notice of where it goes—let yourself pause into the moment.

Validate and Connect With Yourself: Fostering a Healthy Self-Image Through Positive Self-Talk

Many of us don't realize that the words we say have the power to shape who we are in drastic ways. What you tell yourself will impact the way you go out into the world, and it will influence the extent to which you believe in yourself. Self-talk can either bring peace to your mind or sabotage you by causing stress. That's why it matters what you choose to allow yourself to think about the type of person you are. Your self-image shapes every aspect of your life, and it also affects how you relate to the world around you. Perhaps, the most important form of communication is the dialogue that you regularly have with yourself. You're the person that you can't avoid or get away from, so the thoughts that you believe, together with the words that you speak to and about yourself, are important.

Our self-talk habits are perpetuated by the experiences we've had in life. It's in the way we grow up hearing our parents speak about us, the things we believe about ourselves based on other people's opinions, and how we measure our worth against the world's standards, and so many more things. Unfortunately, self-talk patterns tend to be negative and uninspired. We are inclined to believe the worst about ourselves rather than noticing and celebrating the good. It's human nature to accept negative vibrations as a default setting. Luckily, we can actively work to change that view of ourselves and begin to adopt healthier ways of addressing ourselves.

Your inner dialogue matters and learning how to turn your words into positive affirmations and healing mantras will transform the way you communicate with yourself. Subsequently, it will also change how you talk to others. To adopt a more positive self-talk pattern, you can share morning mantras and evening affirmations with yourself. Your brain needs repetition to begin believing things, so wake up each morning and remind yourself of how incredibly capable you are. Tell yourself all the good things that you need to know to make you feel more confident about tackling the day ahead. Starting your day with positive words such as, "I'm doing my best, and that matters" or "Today is going to be great, regardless of what I face," can get you feeling pumped and prepared to meet the day with grit and enthusiasm.

Alternatively, you can use the rubber band method to help you catch and stop negative thoughts throughout the day. It is a trick used in therapy to help you notice and address random thoughts that may be increasingly damaging to your day (Scott, n.d.). Using the rubber band strategy involves wearing a band around your wrist and pulling it back from your skin, and letting it snap on you as a way of paying attention to a negative thought. When you can make a habit of catching yourself ruminating (or having negative thoughts), it's great to stop them before they develop into something more powerful or something that you begin to believe. Also, using this method helps you become more disciplined in limiting the number of negative thoughts that you allow to roam your mind. It may cause slight discomfort to feel the rubber snap on your skin, but over time it will help reduce ineffective thinking. Eventually, those negative ideas will no longer consume you with anxiety and make it difficult for you to communicate with others. Whatever chance you get to improve your inner dialogue, is one worth taking because your relationship with yourself will guide your external relationships—so make it positive.

All That You Are Influences Your Relationships

Cultivating a healthy self-relationship is the beginning of communicating well with others. You treat people with the same respect and attention you give to yourself. Taking into account how important your relationship with yourself is should inspire you to want to do things that make you happy. If you enjoy taking walks, then go on more of those. If you enjoy reading books, then stock up on new material as often as you can. By investing in yourself, you're investing in your relationships as well, and also in the people around you. You don't need to do extravagant things to care for yourself. The simplest decisions like cleaning your space, going to sleep early, eating healthy meals, and keeping good hygiene are forms of self-care, too. Treat yourself like someone you're trying to impress and care for yourself to high standards, this way you won't accept any less treatment from anyone else around you. When you take care of your needs, it improves your mental health and helps you to be a better communicator.

Conclusion

Good communication takes work, effort, and commitment. You must desire to do better, ask for help, collaborate, and listen to what other people have to share. To be an effective communicator you need to value the qualities of listening, validating, and bonding with other people. In valuing these qualities, it's important to understand that communication is about what you can learn from the other person rather than what you can say or how many things you can get right. The road toward becoming a cohesive and effective communicator is paved with patience, empathy, and a willingness to hear others out. Pay attention to the words and nonverbal cues that people share during a conversation and respond to every encounter with kindness.

Most importantly, any strong and fulfilling relationship begins with a healthy version of yourself. You need to care for your body and mind before you can communicate effectively. Your work and home responsibilities can only be accomplished when you're okay. So, take care of yourself with the techniques that you've been given in this book. Lean into all the multiple ways that you can safely confront your social anxiety so you can cultivate better and more satisfying interpersonal relationships. You're far more capable of being a good communicator than you even know, so just keep practicing and believing in your ability to improve.

As you work to become a better version of yourself, I hope that you find delight in listening to people and letting them in. Communication is about connection, so get excited about the opportunity to improve your social skills by drawing closer to people and allowing yourself to learn from your engagements. Also, practice your inner dialogue so that your external encounters can benefit from the positivity and productivity that you've already cultivated in your internal space. Allow self-care and the communication techniques you've read in this book to be your guide as you navigate the multiple ways that you can communicate and connect with people. Make the journey of learning an enjoyable one, and soon your life will be transformed by the wonderful communication skills that you've learned.

References

Abraham, M. (n.d.). *Anxiety and difficulty speaking.* Symptoms. https://www.calmclinic.com/anxiety/symptoms/difficulty-speaking

Ackerman, C. E. (2020, April 1). *What is self-awareness?* (+5 Ways to be more self-aware). Self-Awareness. https://positivepsychology.com/self-awareness-matters-how-you-can-be-more-self-aware/

Anxiety, Fear, and Panic. (n.d.). *Anxiety, fear, and panic.* Mental Health. https://www.nhs.uk/mental-health/feelings-symptoms-behaviours/feelings-and-symptoms/anxiety-fear-panic/

Bailey, C. (2010, June 9). *Listening to what isn't said.* Content. https://www.socialmediatoday.com/content/listening-what-isnt-said

Barot, H. (n.d.). *Ineffective communication explained: And how to avoid it.* Public Speaking. https://franticallyspeaking.com/ineffective-communication-explained-and-how-to-avoid-it/

Beatty, M. J. (2009). *Social and Communicative Anxiety.* Encyclopedia of Communication Theory, 891-92.

Benso, K. (2017, February 26). *The 6 commandments of vulnerable communication.* Healthy Relationships. https://www.huffpost.com/entry/the-6-commandments-of-vulnerable-communication_b_58b286d2e4b0658fc20f967e#:~:text=Vulnerable%20communication%20is%20done%20in,secure%20and%20mutually%20dependent%20relationship

Better Health Channel. (n.d.). *Relationships and communication*. Relationships. https://www.betterhealth.vic.gov.au/health/healthyliving/relationships-and-communication#importance-of-communication

Brooten-Brooks. (2022, January 24). *What is boundary setting?* Mental Health. https://www.verywellhealth.com/setting-boundaries-5208802

Center for Counseling & Mental Health. (n.d.). *10 tips for healthy relationships*. Amherst College. https://www.amherst.edu/campuslife/health-safety-wellness/counseling/self_care/healthy_relationships/10_tips_for_health_relationships

Cherry, K. (n.d.). *5 key emotional intelligence skills*. Personality Psychology. https://www.verywellmind.com/components-of-emotional-intelligence-2795438

Cherry, K. (n.d.). *What is compassion?* Happiness. https://www.verywellmind.com/what-is-compassion-5207366

Cherry, K. (n.d.). *What is self-awareness?* Cognitive Psychology. https://www.verywellmind.com/what-is-self-awareness-2795023

Cirino, E. (n.d.). *Anxiety exercises to help you relax*. Mental Well-Being. https://www.healthline.com/health/anxiety-exercises

Cooks-Campbell, A. (2022, July 14). *Communication is key in the workplace. Here's how to improve*. Collaboration. https://www.betterup.com/blog/why-communication-is-key-to-workplace-and-how-to-improve-skills

Coursera. (n.d.). *Why is workplace communication important? And how to improve it*. Professional Development. https://www.coursera.org/articles/workplace-communication

Cunic, A. (n.d.). *Passive communication and social anxiety*. Social Anxiety Disorder. https://www.verywellmind.com/what-is-passive-communication-3024630

Cunic, A. (n.d.). *What is social anxiety disorder?* Social Anxiety Disorder. https://www.verywellmind.com/social-anxiety-disorder-4157220

Datta, S. (n.d.). *7 most negative effects of poor communication.* Effects of Poor Communication. https://sanjeevdatta.com/effects-of-poor-communication/

Davin, K. (2022, September 12). *Impacts of lack of communication in a relationship & 13 ways to improve.* Lack of Communication In Relationships. https://www.choosingtherapy.com/lack-of-communication-in-a-relationship/

Dickinson, G., & Shipley, R. (n.d.). *Professional communication skills.* Business Courses. https://study.com/learn/lesson/professional-communication-skills.html

Doyle, A. (n.d.). *Verbal communication skills list and examples.* Skills Development. https://www.thebalancemoney.com/verbal-communication-skills-list-2059698

Effective Communication–Improving Your Social Skills. (n.d.). Effective communication–Improving your social skills. https://www.anxietycanada.com/articles/effective-communication-improving-your-social-skills/

Empathetic Listening. (n.d.). *Top Tips for Effective Listening.* Empathetic listening. https://www.skillsyouneed.com/ips/empathic-listening.html

Fletcher, J. (n.d.). *How to practice mindful listening.* Benefits. https://psychcentral.com/lib/mindful-listening-exercise

Gardner, E. (2022, May 7). *How social anxiety impacts romantic relationships & what to do.* Relationships. https://www.online-therapy.com/blog/how-social-anxiety-impacts-romantic-relationships-what-to-do/

Gelles, D. (n.d.). *How to meditate.* Guides. https://www.nytimes.com/guides/well/how-to-meditate

Gilbertson, T. (2016, February 10). *8 things you have the right to expect from your relationship.* Constructive Wallowing. https://www.psychologytoday.com/us/blog/constructive-wallowing/201602/8-things-you-have-the-right-expect-your-relationship

Goleman, D. (2006). *Emotional intelligence. (*10th Edition*).* Bantam Dell. https://asantelim.files.wordpress.com/2018/05/daniel-goleman-emotional-intelligence.pdf

Gross, M. E., Zedelius, C. M., & Schooler, J. W. (2020). Cultivating an understanding of curiosity as a seed for creativity. *Current Opinion in Behavioral Sciences, 35,* 77-82. https://doi.org/10.1016/j.cobeha.2020.07.015

Gulotta, J. (2022, October 11). *22 tips for how to communicate in a relationship.* Choosing Therapy. https://www.choosingtherapy.com/how-to-communicate-in-a-relationship/

Gupta, S. (n.d.). *How to stop being passive-aggressive.* Spouses & Partners. https://www.verywellmind.com/how-to-stop-being-passive-aggressive-7101014

Hall, K. (2012, April 26). *Understanding validation: a way to communicate acceptance.* Pieces of Mind. https://www.psychologytoday.com/za/blog/pieces-mind/201204/understanding-validation-way-communicate-acceptance

Hall, B. (2020, January 15). *Self-care: Building a strong relationship with yourself.* https://discoverinterpreting.org/2020/01/15/building-strong-relationship-with-yourself/

Harmon, E. (n.d.). Why is professional communication important in the workplace? https://www.opencolleges.edu.au/blog/2020/06/05/professional-communication-in-the-workplace/

Heston-Davis, R. (2022, November 9). *How to have a healthy relationship with yourself and why it matters.* Tips for A Good Relationship With Yourself. https://psychcentral.com/health/healthy-relationship-with-yourself#recap

How to improve your emotional intelligence in the workplace. (2022, August 24). How to improve your emotional intelligence in the workplace. Best Practices. https://practice.do/blog/emotional-intelligence-in-the-workplace

How to Meditate. (n.d.). How to meditate. Mindful. https://www.mindful.org/how-to-meditate/

Human Performance Resources. (2022, September 6). *Validation: Show you're listening—even if you disagree.* Relationship Building. https://www.hprc-online.org/social-fitness/relationship-building/validation-show-youre-listening-even-if-you-disagree

Jimenez, J. (2021, July 16). *Compassion vs. empathy: Understanding the difference.* Well-Being. https://www.betterup.com/blog/compassion-vs-empathy

Johnston, E. (n.d.). *What are 'I feel' statements?* Relationships. https://www.verywellmind.com/what-are-feeling-statements-425163

Khillar, S. (2018, May 31). *Difference between pillar and column.* Difference Between Similar Terms and Objects. http://www.differencebetween.net/language/words-language/difference-between-pillar-and-column/

Laderer, A. (2020, July 10). *Shake it off—and other quick physical ways to squash anxiety.* Health. https://greatist.com/health/physical-anxiety-techniques

Manson, M. (n.d.). *Vulnerability: The key to better relationships.* Relationships. https://markmanson.net/vulnerability-in-relationships

Martins, J. (2022, November 14). *12 tips for effective communication in the workplace.* Collaboration.

https://asana.com/resources/effective-communication-workplace

Mazzella, J. (n.d.). *52 Self-care quotes and tiny reminders to love yourself.* Tips & Guides. https://fortuneandframe.com/blogs/news/self-care-quotes

Mental Health Foundation. (n.d.). *Top tips on building and maintaining healthy relationships.* Healthy Relationships. https://www.mentalhealth.org.uk/our-work/public-engagement/healthy-relationships/top-tips-building-and-maintaining-healthy-relationships

Merriam-Webster. (n.d.). *Communication.* In the Merriam-Webster.com dictionary. Retrieved date from April 3, 2023. https://www.merriam-webster.com/dictionary/communication

Murphy, A. (2021, May 27). *What is self-awareness (and how to cultivate it).* Mindfulness. https://declutterthemind.com/blog/self-awareness/

National Institute of Neurological Disorders and Stroke. (n.d.). *Brain basics: understanding sleep.* Health. https://www.ninds.nih.gov/health-information/public-education/brain-basics/brain-basics-understanding-sleep

Nash, J. (2018, January 5). *How to set healthy boundaries & build positive relationships.* Positive CBT. https://positivepsychology.com/great-self-care-setting-healthy-boundaries/

Orr, M. (2021, April 27). *The value of empathy and emotional intelligence at work.* Engagement. https://risepeople.com/blog/empathy-and-emotional-intelligence-at-work/

Patterson, R. (2020, May 1). *The beginner's guide to professional communication.* College Info Geek Community. https://collegeinfogeek.com/professional-communication-guide/

Relationships And Communication. (n.d.). Relationships and communication. Relationships. https://www.betterhealth.vic.gov.au/health/healthyliving/relationships-and-communication

Robbins, T. (n.d.). *How to use "I-statements".* Love & Relationships. https://www.tonyrobbins.com/love-relationships/words-matter-you-vs-i/

Robbins, T. (n.d.). *How to communicate in a relationship.* Ultimate Relationship Guide. https://www.tonyrobbins.com/ultimate-relationship-guide/key-communication-relationships/

Rosaria, D. L., Giulia, V., Giulia, S., & Paola, F. (2019). Emotional intelligence, empathy, and alexithymia: A cross-sectional survey on emotional competence in a group of nursing students. *Acta Bio Medica: Atenei Parmensis, 90*(Suppl 4), 32-43. https://doi: 10.23750/abm.v90i4-S.8273.

Salters, K. (n.d.). *What is emotional validation?* BPD. https://www.verywellmind.com/what-is-emotional-validation-425336

Sander, V. (2022, March 23). *75 social anxiety quotes that show you are not alone.* Mental Well-Being. https://socialself.com/blog/social-anxiety-quotes/

Sands, L. (2021, October 14). *What is informal communication?* Employee Engagement. https://www.breathehr.com/en-gb/blog/topic/employee-engagement/what-is-informal-communication

Schmitz, T. (2016, May 16). *Empathy—the cornerstone of emotional intelligence.* Emotional Intelligence. https://www.conovercompany.com/empathy-the-cornerstone-of-emotional-intelligence/

Scott, E. (n.d.). *18 effective stress relief strategies.* Management Techniques. https://www.verywellmind.com/tips-to-reduce-stress-3145195

Scott, E. (2022, May 24). *Reduce stress and improve your life with positive self talk*. Management Techniques. https://www.verywellmind.com/how-to-use-positive-self-talk-for-stress-relief-3144816

Sharma, D. (2023, February 1). *5 skills needed for effective verbal communication in the workplace*. Verbal Communication Blog. https://www.risely.me/skills-for-verbal-communication-in-the-workplace/

Smith, S. (2021, February 18). *How to improve understanding in a relationship*. Expert Blogger. https://www.marriage.com/advice/relationship/understanding-relationships/

The 10 Principles Of Listening. (n.d.). *The 10 principles of listening*. Top Tips for Effective Listening. https://www.skillsyouneed.com/ips/listening-principles.html

The Vibe Team. (2022, May 5). *35 quotes about communication for inspiring team collaboration*. Blog. https://vibe.us/blog/35-quotes-about-communication/

What Is Empathy? (n.d.). *What is empathy?* Types of empathy. https://www.skillsyouneed.com/ips/empathy.html

Zafar, Z. (2019, May 10). *Communication*. Medium. https://medium.com/@zahrazafarullah786/communication-3d612d633daf

Zenefits Team. (2022 September 22). *36 workplace communication quotes to inspire your team*. Employee Development. https://www.zenefits.com/workest/workplace-communication-quotes/

Printed in Great Britain
by Amazon